T

PSYCHOLOGY OF READING AND SPELLING

WITH SPECIAL REFERENCE TO DISABILITY

By ARTHUR I. GATES

Associate Professor of Education
Teachers College, Columbia University

TEACHERS COLLEGE, COLUMBIA UNIVERSITY
CONTRIBUTIONS TO EDUCATION, NO. 129

PREFACE

THE investigation here reported was made possible by the generosity of Mr. Frank A. Vanderlip, founder of the Scarborough School at Scarborough, New York. Under the supervision of Mr. Wilford M. Aikin, the director of the school, a department of educational research was organized in the school, in the fall of 1920. The writer was placed in charge of the department and throughout has enjoyed the able assistance of Miss Jessie La Salle in conducting tests and examinations and of Miss Theodosia Bay and Miss Ella Woodyard in the statistical treatment of results. To the director and to the members of the staff of the school, the writer is deeply indebted for heartiest coöperation.

Acknowledgment of very helpful suggestions and criticisms are gratefully rendered to Dr. G. S. Gates, Dr. L. S. Hollingworth and Dr. H. L. Hollingworth, each of whom has read the manuscript.

A. I. G.

CONTENTS

Contents

CHAPTER I

INTRODUCTION

Cases of disability or serious difficulty in reading or spelling among children otherwise competent and without discoverable physical defects have been reported from time to time by teachers, physicians, neurologists, opthalmologists and psychologists. The radical differences in diagnoses made by these several workers, although each has instruments and methods of value, betray the inadequacy of the technique for dealing with such cases and the need for further study.

It is the purpose of this report to consider briefly the growth of representative types of study, to describe a method of diagnostic procedure and the main results of its use on a number of cases, together with such suggestions concerning specific remedial treatment and general methods of instruction as were developed during the course of the work.

To trace completely the development of the instruments and technique now used by students of difficulties in reading and spelling, would necessitate a survey of the history of experimental psychology in nearly all its branches. On the one hand, such studies are largely dependent upon the development of tests for general intelligence, for specific mental processes, for achievement in reading and other school functions, as well as the statistical methods involved. On the other hand, the development of laboratory apparatus and technique has made important contributions.

Physiologists, neurologists and opthalmologists as well as psychologists have furnished facts and methods of value. In fact the competent student of educational difficulties should utilize the contributions of these and other branches of science.

In reviewing the investigations in these fields, a sharp contrast of methods of study appears. There are numerous researches in reading and spelling in which the group method has been used exclusively, a smaller but appreciable number of studies by means of individual examinations, but very few in which the two have been combined. Both group and individual methods have their advantages and limitations; each may serve, in many instances, as a profitable supplement to the other.

The facts of individual differences disclose the necessity of measuring a fair sampling of cases in order to establish norms with reference to which the individual before us may be understood. Examinations profit us little without a knowledge of the distribution of traits in the group. Group methods, by means of modern technique of simple, partial and multiple correlations, provide, moreover, for rather precise analyses but only under certain conditions. The investigator must be constantly reminding himself of the assumptions upon which measures of relationship are based and of the uncertainty of interpretation of coefficients as they usually appear. In any extensive series of measurements, instances will quite surely be found in which the method of correlation is inappropriate. If the group is very small or highly selected, interpretation becomes insecure. More subtle difficulties depend upon the character of the relationship when the more obvious requirements are met. For example, the correlation between visual acuity and reading ability is found to be but slightly above zero.[1] That is to say, the average association of reading ability with visual acuity is slight when the whole group is considered. Within the lower quartile of visual acuity, the association may be of great importance. Until correlational methods are adapted to irregular as well as rectilinear relations, group methods must be supplemented by study of selected cases, particularly for purposes of analysis and diagnosis.[2]

When the technical prerequisites of correlation are fulfilled and coefficients are fairly high, the study of individual cases frequently adds information otherwise concealed by the general trend of association in the group. The *causes* of correlation are not easily determined. For example, the Thorndike-McCall Reading Scale gives about the same correlation with a composite of tests of *rate* of reading as many tests which professedly measure rate. The performances of a number of very slow readers gave convincing evidence that the scores in the former test are not determined by the speed

---

[1] See Ruediger, W. C., *The Field of Distinct Vision*, Archives of Psychology, No. 5, 1907, p. 61.

[2] For a discussion of several illustrative instances see Thorndike, E. L., "Fundamental Theorems in Judging Men," *Journal of Applied Psychology*, March 1918, and *Teachers College Record*, May 1918.

of reading, whereas in the others this is the determining factor.[1] The study of cases whose disabilities are known is a fruitful method of ascertaining the validity of tests and measures.

Not least in importance among the services of a combined individual and statistical attack is the possibility of analysis of school functions into their constituent elements. Until the enormously complicated function, reading or spelling, is analysed into its elemental abilities or bonds, there is little hope for the construction of scientifically valid methods of learning or teaching. We need to know precisely what goes on in the bodily mechanisms of a subject when he reads or spells. A promising way of attempting to secure these facts is to ascertain what elements are ineffective or defective when a subject cannot learn or has marked difficulty in learning. Persistent search may eventually provide cases of failure to learn because of disability or defect of each of the constituent abilities. With this information at hand, we shall be able to proceed to formulate intelligently economical and effective methods of instruction. (In education, as in medicine and elsewhere, diagnosis must precede specific treatment.) The success of a certain type of treatment does not verify the diagnosis necessarily nor does the failure of remedial treatment disprove the diagnosis. The good physician observes the beneficial results of general treatment for many diseases which he cannot identify and he diagnoses many diseases for which he has no treatment. In these well known facts are contained cautions, which the educational diagnostician may well observe, for without doubt the present decade will witness the development of practices of diagnosis and treatment of educational ills of many varieties.

[1] See Gates, A. I., "An Experimental and Statistical Study of Reading and Reading Tests," *Journal of Educational Psychology*, Oct., Nov., Dec., 1921.

CHAPTER II

HISTORICAL SURVEY OF REPRESENTATIVE STUDIES OF INDIVIDUAL DIFFICULTIES IN READING AND SPELLING

In the long history of the experimental study of reading and spelling, two investigations stand out as of paramount importance: the work of Javal in 1878,[1] which led to the modern apparatus for recording eye movements, and the work of Cattell in 1885,[2] upon the nature of perceptual reactions in reading. Out of these two related researches, made in the recesses of the psychological laboratory, has grown a host of studies whose results have, within the last decade, wrought important changes in the pedagogy of these subjects. To review even the most important of these studies cannot be attempted in this chapter and is, indeed, unnecessary because it has been ably done elsewhere. In the Appendix will be found a selected list of references to the most important experimental investigations together with certain general accounts summarizing these researches as well as others employing group methods and experimental instruction. The present chapter will be confined to those studies which deal primarily with the diagnosis of particular cases of backwardness and disability. No attempt will be made to summarize systematically the results of these; certain samples of the several types of approach will be presented in some detail.

Historically, medical men, especially neurologists and opthalmologists, were the first to make studies of individual cases of inability to read or spell. The final diagnoses were usually "congenital word-blindness" or "alexia," "congenital aphasia," or "mind-blindness." Almost invariably the assumption was made that "visual memories of words, letters, and figures are deposited in different areas of the cerebral cortex"[3] and that if no ocular or obvious organic defects or lack of intelligence were found, the indication was that the cortical areas were congenitally defective. Precise tests of reading ability,

[1] Javal, E., "Sur la physiologie de la lecture," *Annales d'Oculistique*, 1878.
[2] Cattell, J. McKeen, "Ueber die Zeit der Erkennung und Benennung von Schriftzeichen, Bildern und Farben," *Philos. Studien*, 1885, p. 635–50.
[3] Hinshelwood, J., *Letter-, Word-, and Mind-Blindness*, 1902.

intelligence or any other mental functions were seldom used. The prognosis for such cases was generally assumed to be rather hopeless although various "exercises" were usually advised, frequently designed to strengthen other cortical areas, such as those governing "muscle memories." In all of these studies very little effort was made to analyze reading into its constituent elements. The analytical contributions were almost entirely based upon deductions from the results of definitely localized cortical lesions. The possibility that inhibiting habits, however acquired, may be at the bottom of inability to learn to read was never seriously considered.[4]

In 1917, Bronner published a summary of the earlier work and described a number of cases observed by herself.[5] In case studies this writer has employed a variety of tests of intelligence, perception, memory, form board tests, construction tests, etc., of the sort familiar to the clinical psychologist in addition to a study of the home and school history of the disability. Her findings are summarized in an analysis of the reading process, in which

there are involved (*a*) perception of form and sound, and discrimination of forms and sounds; (*b*) association of sounds with visually perceived letters, of names with groups of symbols and of meanings with groups of words; (*c*) memory; motor visual and auditory; and (*d*) the motor processes, as used in inner speech and in reading aloud. Reviewing the whole process, we see that in the actual performance of reading there must be finally some synthetic process uniting all the separate elements. (p. 78.)

Bronner's diagnoses take such forms as these: "marked deficiency in auditory powers, shown by poor auditory memory and defective discrimination of sound" and "defective auditory perception." As regards remedial treatment it is suggested that "the auditory powers could have been improved by training." Another case presented difficulties in reading said to be due to "defects in visual memory and

<hr>

[4] Historical summaries of the facts and theories produced by this group of workers will be found in the following: Hinshelwood, J., *Congenital Word-Blindness*, London: H. K. Lewis & Co., 1917. Pp. x + 112. Head, H., "Aphasia: an Historical Review," *Brain*, 1920, pp. 390–411. Head, H., "Aphasia and Kindred Disorders of Speech," *Brain*, 1920, pp. 87–165. Current opinions are well expressed in the following articles: Stanley Barnes, J. S. Collier, Henry Head, J. H. Parsons, Sir J. Purves Stewart, and S. A. Kinnier Wilson, "Discussion on Aphasia," *Brain*, 1920, pp. 411–450; and Mourgue, R., "Disorders of Symbolic Thinking due to Local Lesions of the Brain," *British Journal of Psychology* (Medical Section), Jan. 1921.

[5] Bronner, A., *The Psychology of Special Abilities and Disabilities*, pp. vi + 269. Boston: Little, Brown and Co., 1917.

powers of visualization," and the remedy is to make "an effort to develop powers of visualization." In another case, the various mental processes, tested separately, seemed quite normal and lead the author to wonder "whether in reading there is not involved some subtle synthetic process, which at the present time we have not means of studying, but defects of which, nevertheless, are of extreme significance."

Bronner seems to feel confident that "powers of visualization," "auditory powers," and the like can be improved by training but whether this is true of the "synthetic power" or "general language ability" or whether they are to be considered innate and unchangeable like general intelligence is not clear. At any rate, Bronner has not carried her analysis of reading difficulties very far. Her case reports give a large amount of information about general intelligence, "visual memory," "auditory imagery," "recognition memory," "powers of analysis," "apperception," "power to solve problems," etc., but very little information about reading. It is also probably true that except as one is acquainted with the particular tests used, these general "powers" have little of definiteness about them.

Since the publication of Bronner's book on special disabilities, a number of studies of difficulty in reading and spelling have appeared. Sharply different methods of attack are represented among them.

In 1918 L. S. Hollingworth published an intensive study of disabilities in spelling [6] which illustrated a profitable method of attack. The general procedure was: (1) The selection of a group of (15 to 18) children who had experienced difficulty in spelling but were of at least average ability in most other school subjects and in general intelligence. (2) An hour of work daily with the group for twenty weeks during which: (*a*) The physical and temperamental traits of the subjects were studied. (*b*) Their mental functions which might bear upon their deficiencies were examined by means of psychological tests. (*c*) Spelling was taught by a variety of devices. (*d*) Careful records of all products were kept and analysed.

This investigation differed from those of Bronner and others by the use of tests especially devised to meet individual problems rather than the conventional tests of "visual memory" and the like, and

[6] Hollingworth, L. S., *The Psychology of Special Disability in Spelling*, pp. 105. Teachers College: Contributions to Education, No. 88, 1918.

especially in the intensive studies of the types of errors made in oral and written spelling and speech for the purpose of discovering their probable causes. For example, tests were made to ascertain the influence of context on spelling; the constancy of spelling errors; the relative success of efforts to recall the spelling of words compared with efforts to recognize them; the recall of words whose meanings were known as compared to those whose meanings were unknown.

The author comes to the conclusion that infrequent cases who "cannot learn to spell" or "whose ability to spell approaches zero" due to limitations of original nature are to be found. Such a case is designated "special disability." The disability is not due to congenital localized neural lesions or childhood injuries, but it forms "the very fag end of the normal distribution of spelling ability," which is determined by "unknown laws of variation and heredity." They consequently differ in degree but not in kind from normal spellers. It is added that:

By far the greater proportion of the sum total of bad spelling is, however, due to *causes other than special disability* in forming the bonds involved in learning to spell words. Over eighty per cent of the poor spellers in our Experimental Class spelled poorly from some cause other than special disability. General intellectual weakness, lack of interest, distaste for mental drudgery, intellectual inertia, previous learning in a foreign language, sensory defects, and bad handwriting are doubtless the most frequent causes of poor spelling (p. 74).

As a result of the investigation, Hollingworth concludes that the process of learning to spell (or read) a word ordinarily involves the formation of a series of bonds, something like the following:

1. An object, act, quality, etc., is "bound" to a certain sound, which has often been repeated while the object is pointed at, the act performed, etc. In order that the bond may become definitely established it is necessary (a) that the individual should be able to identify in consciousness the object, act, quality, etc., and (b) following that he should be able to recollect the particular vocal sounds which have been associated therewith.

2. The sound (word) becomes "bound" with performance of the highly complex muscular act necessary for articulating it.

3. Certain printed or written symbols, arbitrarily chosen, visually representing sound combinations, become "bound" (a) with the recognized objects, acts, etc., and (b) with their vocal representatives; (so that when these *symbols* are presented to sight, the word can be uttered by the perceiving individual). This is what is called the ability "to read" the word.

4. The separate symbols (letters) become associated with each other in the proper sequence, and have the effect of calling each other up to consciousness in the proper order. When this has taken place, we say that the individual can *spell orally*.

5. The child, by a slow, voluntary process, "binds" the visual perceptions of the separate letters with the muscular movements of hand, arm, and fingers necessary to copy the word.

6. The child "binds" the representatives in consciousness of the visual symbols with the motor responses necessary to produce the written word spontaneously, at pleasure.

Hollingworth's analysis, as she at once points out, is not exhaustive, but it affords a working hypothesis of the constituent elements in reading which is far in advance of the analysis in terms of "visual memory," "auditory imagery" and other "powers." Certainly it is more instructive to the practical worker.

Another line of attack has been developed by the work of Judd and his associates at the University of Chicago. For many years important studies of eye-movements, the eye-voice span, the perceptual process and other factors have been conducted by the aid of elaborate apparatus as well as by the use of standard tests and measures.[1] Several workers have employed these instruments, as well as the conventional devices, in case studies of reading difficulties with promising results.

A recent report by W. S. Gray [8] illustrates the type of procedure. Tests of general mental ability, of achievement in school work, of oral and silent reading, and of visual vocabulary were first given. In the particular case reported, difficulty in pronouncing sight words "suggested a marked weakness in visual memory." This factor was therefore tested by a visual memory exercise. A study was next made of ability to recognize letters, syllables, words and phrases in a tachistoscope and finally photographic records of eye-movements during reading were secured.

The variety of causes of difficulty in reading which he and other present-day workers have found are summarized by Gray in the same article: In the first group mention is made of irregular attend-

[1] Many of these studies are summarized in Judd, C. H., *Reading: Its Nature and Development*, pp. 192. Univ. of Chicago; Supplementary Educational Monograph, Vol. 2, No. 4, 1918.

[8] Gray, W. S., "Diagnostic and Remedial Steps in Reading," *Journal of Educational Research*, June 1921.

ance, poor health, malnutrition, nervous disorders; nationality, inappropriate methods of instruction, inadequate amount of reading, etc. Gray's summary of other causes is quoted:

The organic causes of difficulties in reading are far more difficult to detect and to remedy. Many children experience genuine difficulty because of visual defects.—Some children find it difficult to form the motor coordinations which are essential in reading; carefully prepared exercises to strengthen the muscles of the eyes have proved helpful. A limited visual span prevents some readers from recognizing a group of words at a given fixation. This limitation can be detected through the use of a tachistoscope. Short exposure exercises have proved effective in increasing the amount which one can recognize at a single fixation of the eye. A low degree of visual acuity frequently leads to numerous errors . . . ,

Defects in the brain tissues frequently cause difficulties in reading. Word blindness, for illustration, is defined as extreme difficulty in learning to recognize printed or written language by persons of normal mentality and vision. It has been overcome in a limited number of cases by methods of instruction which make a vigorous appeal to the child. Vocal defects, such as malformations of the vocal organs and enlarged tonsils, interfere seriously with effective reading. Breathing irregularities . . . may lead to errors. Auditory defects frequently lead to errors in pronunciation.

A third group of causes are psychological in character. They include general mental incapacity, inadequate attention to meaning, failure to associate appropriate meanings with words, limited eye-voice span, limited span of recognition, inability to remember new words easily, capacity to learn words only very slowly, forgetting them quickly and easily, and inability to analyse and pronounce words effectively.

The recent studies thus show a great improvement in the technique of investigation, especially in the use of more precise and more elaborate apparatus, and as a consequence a more thorough search through a larger number of functions. The result is the assumption of a wider variety of sources of difficulty and an appreciation of the complexity of the reading with an increase of information concerning its constituent elements. The list of causal factors is doubtless far from complete and contains many factors that are probably not causes at all. Moreover the interrelations of the factors are imperfectly understood and diagnoses are certainly often incorrect.

While "word blindness," defects "in general synthetic ability," or "powers of visualization," "visual memory," "visual imagery," and other rather vague concepts are still found, the tendency is clearly in the direction of more definite diagnosis combined with more specific remedial treatment. Whereas the earlier workers usually gave a discouraging prognosis, many present-day investigators are highly optimistic concerning remedial treatment.

CHAPTER III

GENERAL DESCRIPTION OF THE PRESENT INVESTIGATION

The investigation was conducted chiefly in the Scarborough School, at Scarborough, New York. The pupils of Grades III to VIII inclusive served as subjects. Among them were a number of cases whose difficulties in reading or spelling or both had been unsolved problems for years and to these were added others secured in the city or vicinity of New York.

Any statement of the number of cases representing "serious backwardness," "difficulty," or "disability" will of course be quite arbitrary since no "modes" or lines of demarcation between good and poor appear. About twenty-five cases, all told, were examined who were reported by teachers and appeared on test to experience really serious difficulty or inability in learning.

One hundred and thirty-five students of the Scarborough School were put through all of the group tests and of these 105 completed the individual examinations. From these data were computed norms for the several grades which were used as standards of comparison.

The distribution of those of the subjects who were tested with the Stanford-Binet was as follows:

Stanford I. Q.	80–89	90–99	100–109	110–119	120–129	130–139
Number of Cases	2	8	21	22	19	12

140–149	150–159	160–
2	4	1

The median I. Q. is about 116. Very few were below 100 I. Q.; but two were less than 90. Some of the cases were not tested by the Stanford test, but the scores obtained in other tests indicated that they were of average intelligence or better.

THE TESTS EMPLOYED

I. Tests of General Mental Ability

    1. The Stanford-Binet Mental Age and Intelligence Quotient were secured for all pupils up to and including grade VI and for certain other cases.

2. Group tests of intelligence were given as follows: National Intelligence Test, Forms A and B, grades III to VIII inclusive; Haggerty, Delta 1 or Delta 2, all grades; Otis Primary or Advanced, all grades; Holley Vocabulary Test, all grades; Dearborn, Examination I or II, all grades; Myers Mental Measure, all grades; Illinois Intelligence, all grades; Terman Group Test, grades VII and VIII; and the Army Alpha to certain subjects in grade VIII.

II. TESTS OF ACHIEVEMENT IN SCHOOL SUBJECTS

1. About a dozen tests of reading ability were given to all grades. They are listed below (see III F.).

2. A composite of spelling ability was obtained by combining the results of several tests, aggregating 186 words of varied degrees of difficulty taken from the Ayres-Buckingham List.

3. A composite of arithmetical ability was obtained by combining scores from the Woody Tests (four operations), Monroe's Diagnostic Test (6 to 21 particular tests) and Monroe's Reasoning Test.

4. Handwriting was tested in the usual way by the use of Thorndike's Scale for Quality in Handwriting. A composite score was obtained by multiplying score for quality by letters written per minute.

III. TESTS OF VARIOUS REACTIONS TO VISUAL STIMULI

A. Ability to detect small differences between pairs of printed material; group tests arranged by the writer.
   Test V 1.   Pairs of drawings of objects and geometrical figures.
   Test V 2.   Pairs of groups of six digits.
   Test V 3.   Pairs of non-sense syllables.
   Test V 4.   Pairs of words.

B. Ability to distinguish one printed element from several others of varied resemblance; group tests adapted from various sources.
   Test V 5.   Discrimination of squares, circles, crosses and stars.
   Test V 6.   Discrimination of capital A's.
   Test V 7.   Discrimination of capital K and I's.
   Test V 8.   Discrimination of digits, 2 and 3.

C. Test V 9.   Ability to recognize the correct form of a word among incorrect but similar forms (recognition spelling); arranged by the writer; used as an individual examination.

D. Test V 10. Ability to recognize correct and incorrect forms of words in continuous sense material (proof-reading); group test arranged by the writer.

E. Ability to react to printed words by correct pronunciation.

Test V 11. Ability to pronounce isolated words—individual test arranged by the writer.

Test V 12. Ability to pronounce words in sentences—Gray's Oral Reading Test, individual examination.

F. Ability to react to printed words by awareness of meaning.

Test 13. Single words with correct and incorrect synonyms suggested—group test arranged by the writer.

Test 14. Single words—Holley's Sentence Vocabulary Test.

Test 15. Burgess Reading Test, Form I, given twice.

Test 16. Brown's Reading Test (speed and comprehension tested separately).

Test 17. Courtis Silent Reading Test, No. 2 (speed and comprehension separately), given twice.

Test 18. Monroe's Silent Reading Test (different scoring for speed and comprehension), given twice.

Test 19. Thorndike-McCall Reading Test (comprehension), given two to seven times.

Test 20. Woodworth-Wells' Easy and Hard Directions.

Test 21. Gray's Silent Reading Test, used infrequently.

IV. REACTIONS TO SPOKEN WORDS

Test 22. Ability to react to a spoken word by saying its letters (oral spelling)—test arranged by the writer, individual examination.

Test 23. Ability to react to a spoken word by writing its letters (written spelling)—test arranged by the writer, individual examination.

Test 24. Ability to react to spoken sentences by writing them (spelling to dictation)—group test arranged by the writer.

Test 25. Ability to react to a spoken word by giving its meaning (Stanford-Binet Vocabulary).

Test 26. Ability to comprehend spoken sentences. (Sections of Stanford-Binet.)

V. TESTS OF SENSORY AND MOTOR MECHANISMS AND REACTIONS

Test 27. Tests of hearing (Whipple's *Manual of Physical and Mental Tests*).

Test 28. Tests of vision (Whipple and Tests V 1 to V 8, inclusive)

Tests 29.   Tests of eye movements in reading. (Arranged-passage from Gray's Silent Reading Test used.)

Test 30.   Tests of general motor control (Whipple's *Manual* and Franz, *Handbook of Mental Examination Methods*, Chap. 3).

Test 31.   Speed and quality of writing. (Thorndike Scale.).

Test 32.   Speech defects. (Franz, *Handbook of Mental Examination Methods*, Chap. 4.)

Test 33.   Lip movement and articulation in reading. (Informal.)

Test 34.   The eye-voice span. (Buswell Test.[1])

[1] Buswell, G. T., *An Experimental Study of the Eye-Voice Span in Reading.* Univ. of Chicago, Supplementary Educational Monograph, No. 17, 1920.

STATISTICAL METHODS EMPLOYED

For the most part, the school grade has been used as the group unit. The correlations for the several grades are averaged and the M.D. from the mean of the grade correlations computed. Partial and multiple correlations are based on the average of the grade correlations.

Since the grades are restricted groups, the correlations may not be compared with those obtained from other groups unless the ranges should be the same. In most cases the correlations found for our groups will be smaller than those which would be obtained from unselected children. Since our purpose is to compare one correlation with others obtained from the same group, this attenuation is not a serious defect.

Coefficients of correlation were computed by the Pearson product-moment formula. Partial and multiple correlations were computed by Kelley's method.[2]

OUTLINE OF THE PRESENTATION OF RESULTS

Chapters IV and V include data on the relation of general mental ability and perceptual abilities, respectively, with both reading and spelling. Chapter VI is devoted to an analytical study of reading; Chapter VII to spelling. Chapter VIII, which comprises discussions of the causes of difficulty in the two functions, is in part a summary. A selected list of books and articles for further reading is given in the Appendix.

[2] Kelley, T. L., *Chart to Facilitate the Calculation of Partial Coefficients of Correlation and the Regression Equations.* Stanford University Publications, School of Education, Monograph No. 1, 1921.

CHAPTER IV

THE RELATION OF READING AND SPELLING TO GENERAL MENTAL ABILITY

A. CORRELATIONS OF READING AND SPELLING WITH THREE TYPES OF INTELLIGENCE TESTS

The variables were: (1) Stanford-Binet Mental Age, Grades III to VI; (2) a series of exercises from the group intelligence tests listed in Chapter III, selected by competent judges as being "very verbal";[1] and (3) a series of exercises from group tests judged to be "very nonverbal."[2] Each of these variables required approximately an hour of working time. The variable "reading composite" comprised the scores from the reading tests listed in Chapter III, the range of scores being so arranged that each test was weighted roughly as the square root of the time taken. The variable "spelling composite" was the number of correct spellings from a list of 186 words from various columns of the Ayres-Buckingham Scale.

The data of Table I show that the verbal group tests yield the highest average correlation (0.71) with reading. The correlations of the non-verbal materials which average 0.20 are specially low in Grades VII and VIII. The correlations between the Stanford M.A. and reading rise regularly from 0.30 for Grade III to 0.71 for Grade VI. The number of cases measured by this test in Grades VII and VIII were too few to justify correlations, a fact now greatly regretted because of the interesting grade differences.

The correlations of the verbal group tests with spelling are much lower than those between verbal group and reading; the means are 0.42 and 0.71 respectively. The same is true of the Stanford-Binet, the mean with reading being 0.49 as compared to 0.31 with spelling. The low correlations of the non-verbal tests with spelling and with reading are not reliably different.

[1] The exercises, ranging from the most to the least verbal, are: Dearborn 4, Otis 9, National A2, National B3, Haggerty 1, Otis 7, Illinois 1, National B4, Otis 8, Otis 2, Haggerty 4, Illinois 7, National A4, Dearborn 8 and National A3.

[2] Ranging from the most non-verbal upward on the verbal scale, the exercises are: Dearborn 7, Dearborn 3, Dearborn 9, Myers 3, Myers 4, Haggerty 3, Myers 2, Dearborn 1, Dearborn 6, Illinois 4, National A5, National B5, Dearborn 5 and Illinois 6.

TABLE I

CORRELATIONS OF COMPOSITE OF READING ABILITY

GRADE	WITH STANFORD M. A.	WITH VERBAL GROUP INTELLIGENCE	WITH NON-VERBAL GROUP INTELLIGENCE
III	.30	.70	.15
IV	.35	.60	.24
V	.58	.65	.28
VI	.71	.77	.26
VII	...	.75	.17
VIII	...	.80	.05
MEAN	.49	.71	.20
M. D.	.16	.06	.07

CORRELATIONS OF COMPOSITE OF SPELLING ABILITY

III	.32	.56	.13
IV	.11	.33	.18
V	.37	.26	.21
VI	.45	.43	.18
VII	...	.44	.12
VIII	...	.50	.08
MEAN	.31	.42	.15
M. D.	.11	.08	.04

Reading and spelling are substantially correlated with scores representing a composite of verbal abilities. The justification of applying the term "general intelligence" to such a composite is the fact that achievement in school work and in many vocations and social adjustments is also substantially correlated with such verbal abilities. The relatively high correlation between reading and the verbal group tests is due largely to the fact that achievement in the latter depends greatly upon reading. Inadequacy of reading facility proves to be a great handicap in these tests. The Stanford-Binet in which reading is directly involved to a very slight extent gave I. Q.'s of 120 or more to some of the cases whose I. Q.'s derived from verbal group tests were less than 100. Table II shows illustrative results. Children suffering great difficulty in reading may earn average intelligence on the Stanford-Binet but produce a score equivalent to feeblemindedness on verbal group tests.

TABLE II

I. Q.'s Given by Various Tests to Sampling of Cases of Backwardness
in Rate of Reading

Grade	Subject	Stanford-Binet	N. I. T. A + B	Haggerty	Illinois	Otis	Holley
VIII	L	125+	94	91	89	99	93
VIII	Q	125+	100	99	95	118	103
VI	N	116	90	82	96	100	86
V	K	110	81	72	80	84	68
IV	Q	122	104	74	82	..	82
III	β	122	(Almost complete failure in verbal group tests. I. Q.'s of 50 or less.)				
III	Δ	120	(Almost complete failure in verbal group tests. I. Q.'s of 50 or less.)				
III	X	118, etc.	(Almost complete failure in verbal group tests. I. Q.'s of 50 or less.)				

Among unselected subjects, eliminating cases of mechanical difficulties in reading due to sensory, motor, and other defects, the correlation between reading ability and "general verbal intelligence" would doubtless be higher. In dealing with the backward reader or speller, the first step in diagnosis should be a measure of this general ability and, in our opinion, the Stanford-Binet has no peer for this purpose. The fact that the verbal group tests depend so greatly on *rate* of reading indicates that they fail to give an accurate measure of the general mental ability of the backward readers. There is but one test in the Stanford Scale (Test 4, ten year group) which demands real reading and only one (Dissected Sentences, twelve year group) which requires word recognition.[3] A second reason for using the Stanford-Binet is the fact that its validity, i.e., its correlation with school, vocational and social abilities, is better known. The correlations of non-verbal group tests with all types of school functions and other criteria are so low as to make very uncertain what they really disclose.[4] Finally, the relatively high reliability of the Stanford-Binet favors its use.[5]

[3] Alternatives for these may be offered.
[4] See, for example, Herring, John P., "Verbal and Abstract Elements in Intelligence Examinations," *Journal of Educational Psychology*, Dec. 1921; and Gates, A. I., same journal, March, April, 1922.
[5] See Rugg, H. O. and Colloton, Cecile, "Constancy of the Stanford-Binet as Shown by Retests," *Journal of Educational Psychology*, Sept. 1921.

The achievement in the Stanford-Binet may be taken as at least a rough criterion of expectation for rate and depth of comprehension in reading,—only *roughly* so, for the reason that the correlation of general mental ability and reading is not +1.00, and because our measures of either ability are not perfect. The association, however, is substantial enough to indicate its importance. The reader will remember (see Chapter III) that these results obtain among children of superior endowment, for the most part, and are taken in grade groups. The correlations obtained from an unselected group would doubtless be considerably higher. Corrections for attenuation, due to inadequacy of the measures, would yield a further positive increment.

B. THE MINIMUM INTELLIGENCE REQUISITE FOR READING AND SPELLING

Just what the minimum essential of general mental ability for learning to read is, has not been disclosed with certainty. Tredgold says: "Few imbeciles (I. Q.'s 20 to 50, according to Terman) acquire the power of reading, but the majority of the feebleminded (I. Q.'s 50 to 70 or 75, according to Terman), as a result of training, learn to read books of simple words and sentences." [6]

Terman finds that feebleminded and very dull subjects acquire, quite frequently, the mechanical abilities enabling them to recognize and pronounce the words. Their reading "bears a close analogy to the reading of nonsense matter by the normal person." [7] "A little observation will convince one that mentally retarded subjects, even when they possess a reasonable degree of fluency in recognizing printed words, do not sense shades of meaning. Their reading is by small units. Words and phrases do not fuse into one mental content, but remain relatively unconnected. The expression is monotonous, and the voice has more of the unnatural schoolroom pitch. . . ." "In short, one who has psychological insight and is acquainted with reading standards can easily detect the symptoms of intellectual inferiority by hearing a dull subject read a brief selection," although "they sometimes read the words of the text fairly fluently."

[6] Tredgold, A. F., *Mental Deficiency*, p. 447. New York: William Wood, 1920. See also Burt, Cyril, *Mental and Scholastic Tests*, pp. 283 ff. London: P. S. King, 1921.
[7] Terman, L. M., *The Measurement of Intelligence*, pp. 266 f. Boston: Houghton Mifflin, 1916.

In the present investigation, we have not undertaken a study of the relation of low mentality to reading difficulty, important as such research may be. It is worthy of note, however, that subjects of very low general mental ability succeed in acquiring (some of them without great difficulty) the mechanical abilities involved in reading. The fact that children of average or superior general mental endowment sometimes experience great difficulty in learning, even fail altogether, therefore becomes the more notable.

There is practically no information available concerning the minimal general mental ability requisite for spelling, although among such groups as have been tested positive correlations of various magnitudes have been found.[8] In the following chapters it will be shown that difficulties in spelling are closely associated with those in reading although they are not always identical. In either case, the significance of general mental ability should be carefully considered in diagnostic and remedial work.

The form of instruction in these verbal functions which is best adapted to individuals of low general mental ability has not yet been satisfactorily determined. The authorities seem rather generally to agree that the methods best suited to the normal children are likewise best suited to the dull, "but time and patience rather than any particular method are the chief essentials."[9]

[8] See Hollingworth, L. S., *op. cit.*
[9] Tredgold, *op. cit.*, p. 447. For a summary of principles to be observed in the education of the sub-normal, see Hollingworth, L. S., *The Psychology of Subnormal Children*, Chap. x. New York: Macmillan, 1921.

CHAPTER V

THE PERCEPTUAL ABILITIES INVOLVED IN READING AND SPELLING

When pupils of average or superior intelligence fail to learn to read or spell properly, investigators usually instigate a search at once for defects of vision. Occasionally, they find unsuspected visual deficiencies which are much more easily remedied than difficulty in reading or spelling. Inappropriate perceptual habits acquired during the period of visual inadequacy are sometimes supplanted only as the result of careful and persistent training. Frequently no visual defects are discovered, and deficiencies in "visual perception," "powers of visualization," and the like are often assumed.

Tests V 1 to V 10 inclusive were adapted or devised for the purpose of discovering defects of vision and visual perception, and of providing materials for the study of several perceptual functions involved in dealing with words and other items.

A. DESCRIPTION OF TESTS V 1 TO V 10 INCLUSIVE

TEST V 1. *Ability to detect small differences between pairs of printed figures.* This test consists of 50 pairs of drawings of common objects or geometrical designs of which half of the pairs are identical and half differ in more or less obvious details. Subjects are instructed to draw an X after each pair where the drawings *are not* alike. The procedure is illustrated on the board. Time, one minute. The score is the number right minus the sum of erroneous markings and omissions.

TEST V 2. *Ability to detect small differences between pairs of printed groups of digits.* This test is the same in form as Test V 1, but differs in content. It consists of 25 pairs of groups of 6 digits whose members are unlike in one or two digits, and 75 like pairs. Three minutes were allowed. The score was computed as in Test 1.

TEST V 3. *Ability to detect small differences in pairs of printed non-sense syllables.* This test is the same in form as Tests V 1 and V 2, but the materials are pairs of non-sense words; five pairs of 2 letters, five of 3, etc., up to five of 11, making a total of 50 of which 25 pairs differ in one or more letters; for example:

tz	tx	fosdily	fondily
ams	ans	seclipqer	secliqper
meark	maerk	lewsaqrnuif	lewesqrnuif

Changes were made about equally often in the beginning, middle and end of the combinations of letters. Two minutes were allowed; the results were scored as in Tests V 1 and V 2.

TEST V 4. *Ability to detect small differences in printed pairs of words.* This test was constructed in the same manner as Test V 3 except that familiar words were used. They ranged, in groups of 5, from 2 to 11 letters. They were selected from Jones' lists of words most frequently used in ten primary readers. One minute was allowed and results were scored as in Tests V 1, V 2, and V 3. Samples of the list follow:

he	ha	haycock	haycock
me	me	election	eliction
drive	drine	represent	represant
ground	grourd	neighborly	neaghborly
behind	bekind	wonderfully	wondenfully

TEST V 5. *Ability to distinguish a given geometrical figure from several others.*[1] This test includes four squares of 100 figures in which the circles, stars, crosses and squares, respectively, are cancelled. Time, 1½ minutes. Results scored as in the earlier tests.

TEST V 6. *Ability to distinguish capital A's from other letters.* The material consists of seven hundred letters arranged at random in groups of 5. It is an adaptation of the familiar A test (Woodworth-Wells). Score is the sum of A's cancelled plus other letters not cancelled minus the sum of A's not cancelled and other letters cancelled, as far as the subject went in 1½ minutes.

TEST V 7. *Ability to distinguish groups of five letters containing both K and I from other groups of five letters.* Same time and material as in Test 6. Score is same as in Test 6, except count is made by groups instead of by single letters. This test is an adaptation of the Woodworth-Wells cancellation test.

[1] Tests V5, V6, V7 and V8 are adaptations of the Woodworth-Wells cancellation tests. See Woodworth, R. S. and Wells, F. L., *Association Tests.* Psych. Review Monographs, No. 57, 1911.

TEST V 8. *Ability to distinguish groups of six digits which contain both 2 and 3 from other groups of six digits.* This is the familiar number checking test from Woodworth-Wells. There were 168 groups. Time allowed, 2 minutes. Results were scored as in Test V 7.

TEST V 9. *Ability to recognize the correct form of a word among incorrect but similar forms.* This test consists of a series of 36 words of known spelling difficulty selected from the Ayres-Buckingham list and arranged in order of difficulty. Each word is accompanied by four misspellings which were either phonically or visually partly similar. The correctly spelled words here used are the same as were employed in tests of pronunciation, written and oral spelling to be described later. This test may be given to a group, but in our investigation it was given individually immediately after individual tests of pronouncing, etc., in order to afford the subject no opportunity to study words on which he had failed. The subject was given unlimited time in which to underline the word in each group which was correctly spelled. The score is the number correct.

Samples of the material follow:

6. dey -- day -- dai -- dag -- dah.
15. prisen -- prisson -- prison -- prizen -- prizzen.
25. difficulty -- dificculty -- defficulty -- difikulty -- differculty.
30. maggnifsunt -- magnifersant -- magniffersunt -- magnificent -- magnificant.
36. consensious -- kontientious -- conscientious -- konsienscious -- constientious.

TEST V 10. *Ability to recognize correct and incorrect forms of words in continuous meaningful material.* The task here was to "proof-read" a passage of 532 words which contained 128 misspellings. Practically all of the words used are frequently read or written as indicated by their presence in the Ayres-Buckingham or the Thorndike lists,[2] although the range is from the easiest words like *get* (git) to *conscientious* (conscentious), etc. Different misspellings of a word appear. Three minutes were allowed. In scoring, the method of number of words read minus twice the sum of misspellings unchecked and correct words checked, was arbitrarily adopted to give a moderately heavy penalty to errors.

[2] Thorndike, E. L., *The Teacher's Word Book*. New York: Teachers College, 1921.

B. A STUDY OF VISUAL PERCEPTION OF VARIOUS MATERIALS

1. RESULTS FROM TEST V 1. *Ability to detect small differences between two drawings.* Table III gives the correlations with this test and other tests of reactions to visual stimuli, as well as with reading and spelling. The correlations for each grade are presented, together with the means and M.D.'s from the means.

TABLE III

CORRELATIONS OF THE ABILITY TO DETECT SMALL DIFFERENCES BETWEEN PAIRS OF DRAWINGS (TEST V_1) WITH:

GRADE	V2 DIGITS	V3 NON-SENSE	V4 WORDS	V5 GEOM. FIG-URES	V6 A's	V7 K. I.	V8 2, 3	V9 RECOG. SPELL.	V10 PROOF-READ.	COMP. SPELL-ING	COMP. READ-ING
III	.00	.13	.20	.12	.16	.13	.27	—.19	.21	—.26	—.06
IV	—.13	.05	.06	.28	.07	.11	—.05	.02	.20	.30	.32
V	.29	.34	—.07	.18	.37	.34	.04	—.10	.07	—.07	.12
VI	.14	.13	.20	.30	.20	.26	.08	.25	.28	—.10	.04
VII	—.14	—.03	—.13	.28	.10	—.10	—.08	—.05	.07	—.09	—.05
VIII	.08	—.13	.07	.43	—.11	—.03	—.02	.10	.05	.00	—.10
M	.04	.08	.06	.26	.13	.12	.04	.01	.15	—.04	.05
M. D.	.13	.12	.10	.08	.11	.13	.09	.12	.08	.12	.12

The ability to detect small differences in drawings gives correlations of approximately zero with other tests involving the same form of reaction when the material is digits, non-sense words or meaningful words. The implication is that there is no *general power* of visual discrimination at work in these functions.

Tests V 5, V 6, V 7 and V 8 demand a different type of reaction —that of selecting and "cancelling" a given item in series with other items. The correlations between these and Test V 1 are very near zero in every case except those between Tests V 1 and V 5, where the correlation is 0.26. The explanation is that these two tests have very similar material (geometrical drawings), although the form of reaction is different.

So far as the correlations show, the ability to detect small differences between two drawings is involved neither in reading ($r = 0.05$) nor in spelling ($r = -0.04$). The case illustrates a situation in which the coefficient of correlation, based on rectilinear regression of the scores, fails to disclose the value of a test for diagnostic purposes. The correlation between reading and visual acuity, for example, may be zero because the regression line is not rectilinear and the method of correlation therefore inadequate. A certain visual acuity is essential, but increments of visual acuity beyond the minimum essential may bring no increase to reading ability.

Test V 1 proved to be of value in detecting occasional unsuspected cases of visual difficulty. Since the test can be given to large groups

TABLE IV

SCORES FOR SUBJECTS WITH GLASSES ON AND GLASSES OFF

GLASSES ON, FIRST TRIAL; GLASSES OFF, SECOND TRIAL

SUBJECT	Test V_1 On	Off	Test V_2 On	Off	Test V_3 On	Off	Test V_4 On	Off	Test V_5 On	Off	Test V_6 On	Off
1	18	24	39	35	35	29	29	35	280	400	80	92
2	7	9	20	22	23	18	21	26	200	268	49	49
3	24	35	26	20	27	21	25	27	217	240	26	29
4	16	24	23	22	30	35	30	32	254	260	60	77
5	15	22	30	30	40	45	35	40	250	279	64	72
6	22	38	50	36	42	47	38	39	321	344	65	65
7	21	—2	19	—30	19	0	19	9	190	61	48	—5
8	29	20	26	22	47	19	39	27	384	350	104	77
9	38	10	30	17	50	14	41	13	250	200	60	48
10	36	22	23	18	37	35	35	27	268	278	53	64
11	18	1	28	27	22	9	13	4	315	209	63	35
12	36	24	36	27	50	40	44	35	330	260	103	80
13	24	13	26	19	39	32	26	18	247	220	29	29
14	19	8	26	22	38	30	34	23	200	107	92	72
MEAN	23	18	29	21	36	27	31	33	265	248	64	56
M.D.	6.9	10.3	6.0	8.2	8.2	11.3	9.9	10.1	44.3	64.7	17.7	21.6

in a few minutes' time, it is worth examining for this purpose. That it does disclose at least serious defects is indicated by the data of Table IV which gives the scores obtained by a group of children with and without correction of defects by glasses. Improvement by practice in this test is great, but most of the defects show themselves clearly. Test V 2 (digits) seems to be, in some respects, even better for this purpose, but neither is as refined as might be desired. A new test combining the merits of both will be constructed for future work.

Tests V 3 and V 4 also give low scores when the subject has visual difficulties, but as will be seen later, low scores in these tests result frequently from certain other causes which should not be confused with physical defects.

2. RESULTS FROM TEST V 2. *Ability to detect small differences between two groups of digits.* The correlations are shown in Table V.

TABLE V

CORRELATIONS OF ABILITY TO DETECT SMALL DIFFERENCES BETWEEN TWO SERIES OF DIGITS (TEST V2) WITH:

GRADE	V3 NON-SENSE	V4 WORDS	V5 GEOM. FIG-URES	V6 A's	V7 K.I.	V8 2,3	V9 RECOG. SPELL.	V10 PROOF-READ.	COMP. SPELL-ING	COMP. READ-ING
III	.20	.29	.05	.05	.08	.20	.26	—.26	—.13	.21
IV	.43	.27	.39	.18	.12	.45	.07	.24	—.30	.26
V	.23	.11	.03	.23	.24	.29	.08	.12	.11	.07
VI	.22	.24	.29	.17	.12	.43	—.05	.00	.14	.14
VII	.38	.29	.19	.49	.57	.55	.18	.32	.06	.02
VIII	.14	.02	.19	.27	.27	.64	.05	.11	—.16	.12
MEAN	.27	.20	.19	.24	.23	.43	.10	.09	—.05	.14
M. D.	.09	.09	.10	.10	.13	.12	.08	.15	.15	.07

This test shows a zero correlation with spelling and a correlation of but 0.14 with reading. The highest correlation (0.43) is with Test V 8, which is similar in content (digits) although the task is different. It yields a low but positive correlation with tests of the same task when the content is non-sense syllables or words (Tests V 4 and V 5), but the correlations with tests differing in both form and content (Tests V 9 and V 10) are zero.

The diagnostic value of Test V 2 is similar to that of Test V 1 in detecting visual defects and in providing data concerning visual perception. Now and then are found cases which perform well in Tests V 1 and V 2, less well in Test V 3, and very poorly in Test V 4. This is taken as evidence that the source of trouble is not organic (visual) defect but probably some acquired form of word perception which is unfavorable to reading or spelling. The distinction, for purposes of diagnosis, is most important and will be treated more fully in later sections.

3. RESULTS FROM TESTS V 5, V 6, V 7, V 8. *Ability to distinguish one printed element from several others.* The materials to be underlined were: Test V 5, geometrical figures; Test V 6, A's; Test V 7, groups of letters containing both K and I and Test V 8, groups of digits containing both 2 and 3. Table VI gives the correlations. The coefficients among functions in this group range from 0.24 to 0.58, mean 0.39; the higher correlations are found where the content is similar, i. e., between the A and K and I tests. The correlations of the tests in this group with those in the first group of four vary from 0.04 to 0.43, median 0.20, the highest occurring in cases of similar content. The correlations of Tests V 5 to V 8, with Test V 9 (recognition of correct spelling) and with Test V 10 (proof-reading), range from 0.08 to 0.17. The correlations with spelling range from −0.03 to +0.16; those with reading are similarly but slightly above zero.

Table IV shows that pupils with visual defects in operation due to the removal of glasses, do poorly in all tests, V 1 to V 8.

In certain cases it was also found that a slowness of motor reaction to the various visual stimuli resulted in a low score. Such cases were too few to affect the correlations markedly, but for diagnosis the distinction between visual defect and sluggishness of motor reaction is important. Both should be further investigated. It is frequently possible, however, roughly to differentiate the two by study of the results from these tests for the reason that (1) when the difficulty is visual the number of erroneous reactions is large and (2) when the difficulty is motor, the erroneous reactions are relatively few although the total score may be low.

Low scores in Tests V1 to V 8 are common among subjects with defective balance and control of the eye muscles (*heterophoria* or *heterotropia*). Cases under treatment for strabismus or weakness of certain muscles were given these tests, and usually, but not invariably, received low scores. Defects of eye muscle balance and control are often unsuspected and cannot be distinguished from refractive errors, except by a technical examination. Slow and erroneous reactions in these tests therefore merit more thoroughout examinations of the eyes and of general muscular coördination.[1]

[1] For simple tests, see Whipple, G. M., *Manual of Mental and Physical Tests.* Part I: Simpler Processes, Chaps. v and vi. Baltimore: Warwick and York, 1914. Or Franz, S. I., *Handbook of Mental Examination Methods*, Chap. iii. New York: Macmillan, 1919.

TABLE VI

CORRELATIONS OF TESTS V5, V6, V7 AND V8 WITH EACH OTHER AND
WITH OTHER VARIABLES

TEST V5 (GEOM. FIGURES)

GRADE	V1 FIGURES	V2 DIGITS	V3 NON-SENSE SYLLS.	V4 SENSE WORDS	V5 GEOM. FIGURES	V6 A TEST	V7 K.I. TEST	V8 2,3 TEST	V9 Select Correct Spelling	V10 RECOG. MISPELL.	COMP. SPELLING	COMP. READING
III	.12	.05	.11	.24	...	.13	—.07	.35	.20	.16	.23	.29
IV	.28	.39	.15	.26	...	.50	.32	.57	.01	.22	.12	.08
V	.18	.03	.32	—.07	...	.45	.36	.28	.20	.18	.35	.11
VI	.30	.29	.32	.01	...	.30	.45	.47	.10	.11	.04	.42
VII	.28	.19	.26	—.02	...	.29	.39	.46	.16	.25	—.11	—.14
VIII	.43	.19	.22	.19	...	.22	—.04	.23	.12	.10	.18	.20
MEAN	.26	.19	.23	.10	...	.32	.24	.39	.13	.17	.14	.16
M. D.	.08	.10	.07	.13	...	.11	.18	.11	.06	.05	.12	.14

TEST V6 (A TEST)

GRADE	V1 FIGURES	V2 DIGITS	V3 NON-SENSE SYLLS.	V4 SENSE WORDS	V5 GEOM. FIGURES	V6 A TEST	V7 K.I. TEST	V8 2,3 TEST	V9 Select Correct Spelling	V10 RECOG. MISPELL.	COMP. SPELLING	COMP. READING
III	.16	.05	.19	—.07	.13	...	.62	.38	—.27	—.09	.17	.13
IV	.07	.18	.18	.38	.50	...	.54	.53	.30	.36	.18	.21
V	.37	.23	.25	.18	.45	...	.71	.41	.20	.15	.14	—.02
VI	.20	.17	.27	.40	.30	...	.45	.40	.26	.12	.07	.15
VII	.10	.49	.31	.05	.29	...	.63	.57	.13	.23	.44	.26
VIII	—.11	.29	.08	—.12	.22	...	.51	.48	.16	.19	.00	.12
MEAN	.13	.24	.21	.14	.32	...	.58	.46	.13	.16	.17	.14
M. D.	.11	.11	.06	.18	.11	...	.08	.07	.13	.16	.10	.07

TEST V7 (K. I. TEST)

GRADE	V1 FIGURES	V2 DIGITS	V3 NON-SENSE SYLLS.	V4 SENSE WORDS	V5 GEOM. FIGURES	V6 A TEST	V7 K.I. TEST	V8 2,3 TEST	V9 Select Correct Spelling	V10 RECOG. MISPELL.	COMP. SPELLING	COMP. READING
III	.13	.08	.01	.02	—.07	.62	...	.08	.04	—.33	.19	—.05
IV	.11	.12	.41	—.32	.32	.54	...	.49	.36	.32	.28	.04
V	.34	.24	.42	.09	.36	.71	...	.26	.12	.10	—.03	.09
VI	.26	.12	.04	.30	.45	.45	...	.35	.28	.18	—.04	.09
VII	—.10	.57	.27	.15	.39	.63	...	.66	.12	.19	—.16	—.04
VIII	—.03	.27	.24	.03	—.04	.51	...	.24	.08	.06	.00	.10
MEAN	.12	.23	.23	.05	.24	.58	...	.35	.17	.09	.04	.04
M. D.	.13	.13	.14	.14	.18	.08	...	.15	.10	.15	.13	.06

TEST V8 (2, 3, TEST)

GRADE	V1 FIGURES	V2 DIGITS	V3 NON-SENSE SYLLS.	V4 SENSE WORDS	V5 GEOM. FIGURES	V6 A TEST	V7 K.I. TEST	V8 2,3 TEST	V9 Select Correct Spelling	V10 RECOG. MISPELL.	COMP. SPELLING	COMP. READING
III	.27	.20	.09	—.03	.35	.38	.08	...	—.08	.04	.11	.19
IV	—.05	.45	.46	.29	.57	.53	.49	...	.30	.23	.05	.11
V	.04	.29	.27	.31	.28	.41	.26	...	.12	.18	—.09	.23
VI	.08	.43	.25	.07	.47	.40	.35	...	—.13	—.14	—.18	.23
VII	—.08	.55	.19	.07	.46	.57	.66	...	.17	.24	.00	—.08
VIII	—.02	.64	.20	—.05	.23	.48	.24	...	.10	.12	—.04	—.03
MEAN	.04	.43	.24	.11	.39	.46	.35	...	.08	.11	—.03	.11
M. D.	.09	.12	.08	.13	.11	.07	.15	...	.13	.11	.08	.11

Infrequently, low scores in these tests seem to be associated with what we conventionally call "inadequacy of attention." A few of our subjects were "flighty," unable or unwilling to work persistently, frequently making halts on diverse pretences. The problem of nervous and emotional instability will be considered briefly in Chapter VIII. At this point it is only necessary to say that these cases must be tested individually, and usually for shorter periods, in order to secure valid information concerning vision and motor control.

Eliminating visual defects, motor inadequacy, instability and other causes (ill health, fatigue, etc.) of inferior performance in these tests, there remains the possibility of defects in "general perceptual ability."

TABLE VII

AVERAGES OF THE CORRELATIONS FOR GRADES III TO VIII INCLUSIVE
BETWEEN TESTS V1 TO V8 INCLUSIVE

TESTS	V1 PICTURES	V2 DIGITS	V3 NON-SENSE	V4 WORDS	V5 FIGURES	V6 A's	V7 K.I.	V8 2, 3
V1 pictures	...	.04	.08	.06	.26	.13	.12	.04
V2 digits	.04	...	.27	.20	.19	.24	.23	.43
V3 non-sense	.08	.27	...	.46	.23	.21	.23	.24
V4 words	.06	.20	.46	...	.10	.14	.05	.11
V5 figs.	.26	.19	.23	.10	...	.32	.24	.39
V6 A's	.13	.24	.21	.14	.32	...	.58	.46
V7 K.I.	.12	.23	.23	.05	.24	.58	...	.35
V8 2, 3	.04	.43	.24	.11	.39	.46	.35	...
MEAN	.10	.23	.25	.16	.25	.30	.26	.30

Table VII shows the averages of the several grade correlations between the various perception tests. It should be recalled that these correlations would be lower than they are if the cases of visual defects, motor defects, inappropriate attention, etc., which affect all those functions similarly had been eliminated. Even with these cases included, the correlations of any one test with others are very low. They are highest in cases of similar content, i. e., V 1 with V 5 V 2 and V 8, V 3 and V 4, V 6 with V 7. It is clearly not the form of the function which produces correlation; in other words, there does not appear to be any such thing as "general visual perception." Rather there are abilities to perceive words, digits, geometrical figures, etc.; each of which is relatively independent of other perceptual abilities.

These facts are borne out by a detailed study of poor readers and spellers. We have not found a single case in which poor reading and spelling were associated with generally inferior perception. Low scores in the perception tests, among our subjects, were due to defects of vision, eye-motor control, general motor control, inattentiveness, instability or something other than general perceptual difficulty.

The importance of making these distinctions with care lies in the fact that remedial treatment will doubtless be different for the several types of difficulty.

C. AN ANALYSIS OF ABILITIES INVOLVED IN PERCEPTION OF WORDS

1. RESULTS FROM TESTS V 3 and V 4. *Ability to detect small differences between two non-sense words (Test V 3) and between two senseful words (Test V 4).* The correlations are given in Table VIII. These tests, it will be recalled, are the same in form as Tests V 1 and V 2, differing in the material used. The correlations between Test V 3 (non-sense) and V 1 (pictures) is 0.08; between Test V 3 and V 2 (digits), 0.27. The correlations of Test V 4 (words) with V 1 is 0.06 and with V 2, 0.20. The correlation between Test V 3 (non-sense) and V 4 (words) is much higher, 0.46.

It will be recalled also that Tests V 1, V 2, V 5, V 6, V 7 and V 8 gave approximately zero or very low correlations with both reading and spelling. Test V 3 (non-sense) gives a correlation of 0.27 with reading and 0.35 with spelling; Test V 4 (words) gives a correlation of 0.39 with reading and 0.55 with spelling. The correlation of Test V 4 with Test V 9 (recognition of a correctly spelled word in a group of misspellings) is 0.47 and the correlation between Test V 4 and V 10 (proof-reading) is 0.56. All correlations between abilities to react to words in various ways are positive and fairly high. The correlations of all these abilities to react to words with the ability to detect small differences in non-sense material are positive, but less high. Correlations between abilities to deal with words and similar abilities to deal with figures, geometrical designs, single letters and digits are very low. These results are summarized for convenience of inspection in Table IX.

TABLE VIII

CORRELATIONS OF ABILITY TO DETECT SMALL DIFFERENCES BETWEEN TWO NON-SENSE WORDS (TEST V 3) AND ABILITY TO DETECT SMALL DIFFERENCES BETWEEN TWO SENSEFUL WORDS (TEST V 4) WITH OTHER VARIABLES

TEST V 3 (NON-SENSE) WITH:

GRADE	V 1 Fig-ures	V 2 Dig-its	V 3 Non-Sense	V 4 Words	V 5 Geo-metrical Fig-ures	V 6 A	V 7 K. I.	V 8 2, 3	V 9 Recog-nition Spell.	V 10 Proof Read.	Com-posite Spell-ing	Com-posite Read-ing
III	.13	.20	...	.40	.11	.19	.01	.49	.44	.33	.24	.13
IV	.05	.43	...	.25	.15	.18	.41	.46	.40	.20	.32	.55
V	.34	.23	...	.38	.32	.25	.42	.27	.30	.26	.44	.27
VI	.13	.22	...	.60	.32	.27	.04	.25	.21	.43	.32	.23
VII	-.03	.38	...	.53	.26	.31	.27	.19	.28	.54	.43	.19
VIII	.13	.14	...	.59	.22	.08	.24	.20	.30	.34	.36	.27
MEAN	.08	.27	...	.46	.23	.21	.23	.24	.32	.35	.35	.27
M. D.	.12	.19	...	.11	.07	.06	.14	.08	.07	.09	.06	.09

TEST V 4 (WORDS) WITH:

GRADE	V 1 Fig-ures	V 2 Dig-its	V 3 Non-Sense	V 4 Words	V 5 Geo-metrical Fig-ures	V 6 A	V 7 K. I.	V 8 2, 3	V 9 Recog-nition Spell.	V 10 Proof Read.	Com-posite Spell-ing	Com-posite Read-ing
III	.20	.29	.40	...	.24	.07	.02	-.03	.58	.36	.57	.60
IV	.09	.27	.25	...	.26	.38	-.32	.29	.40	.60	.51	.20
V	.07	.11	.38	...	.07	.18	.09	.31	.44	.49	.42	.36
VI	.20	.24	.60	...	.01	.40	.30	.07	.32	.62	.44	.40
VII	-.13	.29	.53	...	.02	.05	.15	.07	.56	.08	.68	.41
VIII	.07	.02	.59	...	.19	-.12	.03	-.05	.56	.58	.67	.42
MEAN	.06	.20	.46	...	.10	.14	.05	.11	.47	.50	.55	.39
M. D.	.10	.09	.12	...	.13	.18	.14	.13	.08	.09	.09	.08

A consideration of the r's for Tests V 1, V 2, V 3, and V 4, in which the same form of task is set, is specially instructive. The mere form of the function "ability to detect small differences between pairs of visual objects" seems to have no association with reading or spelling, but the ability to detect small differences in *words* shows a

TABLE IX

CORRELATIONS OF SPELLING AND READING WITH OTHER VARIABLES.
r IS THE MEAN OF THE *r*'s FOR GRADES III TO VIII

	SPELLING	READING	RECOGNITION SPELLING	PROOF READING
Test V 1, small differences in drawings	—.04	.05	.01	.15
Test V 2, small differences in digits . .	—.05	.14	.01	.09
Test V 5, cancelling geometric figures .	.14	.16	.13	.17
Test V 5, cancelling A's	.17	.14	.13	.16
Test V 6, cancelling K. I.	.04	.04	.17	.09
Test V 8, cancelling 2, 3	.03	.11	.08	.11
Test V 3, small differences, non-sense .	.35	.27	.32	.35
Test V 4, small differences, words . .	.55	.39	.47	.56

fairly high correlation. This leads us to the hypothesis that success in reading and spelling is dependent upon some ability to perceive clearly the significant features of words.

In the following sections, this hypothesis will be tested by the use of other tests and experiments.

2. RESULTS FROM TEST V 9. *Ability to recognize the correct spelling of a word among incorrect spellings.* This test (described above) consists of 36 words, giving a range of difficulty, each word arranged with four misspellings on a line. The subject underlined the word considered to be correctly spelled.

Table X gives the correlations of this test with the other variables previously considered. The highest correlation is that with the composite of spelling 0.63. The correlation of recognition spelling with recall (oral spelling) of the same list of words is 0.65. The next highest correlation is with proof-reading (Test V 10), which averages 0.53. The correlation of recognition spelling with the composite of reading (0.47) is the same as that with ability to detect small differences in words; that between recognition spelling and detecting differences between non-sense words is 0.32. The correlations of recognition spelling with other functions of the perceptual type are zero or slightly positive.

Since the correlation of this test with proof-reading is fairly high, and both show positive correlations with other functions involving words, it will be an economy of space to consider the two, together with others, in the next section.

TABLE X

CORRELATION OF TEST V9, RECOGNITION OF SPELLING OF A WORD, WITH:

GRADE	V 1 FIGURES	V 2 DIGITS	V 3 NON-SENSE	V 4 WORDS	V 5 GEOM. FIGURES	V 6 A's	V 7 K. I.	V 8 2, 3	V 10 PROOF-READING	COMPOSITE SPELLING	COMPOSITE READING
III	—.19	.26	.44	.58	.20	—.27	.04	—.08	.80	.80	.74
IV	.02	.07	.40	.40	.01	.30	.36	.30	.30	.44	.50
V	—.10	.08	.30	.44	.20	.20	.12	.12	.67	.57	.40
VI	.25	—.05	.21	.32	.10	.26	.28	—.13	.38	.71	.22
VII	—.05	.18	.28	.56	.16	.13	.12	.17	.49	.59	.44
VIII	.10	.05	.30	.50	.12	.16	.08	.10	.55	.68	.51
MEAN	.01	.10	.32	.47	.13	.13	.17	.08	.53	.63	.47
M. D.	.12	.08	.07	.08	.06	.13	.10	.13	.14	.10	.11

3. RESULTS FROM TEST V 10. *Ability to detect misspellings in connected sense material—"proof-reading."* This test consisted of a passage of 532 words of which 128 were misspelled. The task was to "draw a line under every word that *is not correctly spelled.*"

Table XI gives the correlations. The highest correlation is with Test V 4, the ability to detect small differences in words (0.56),

TABLE XI

CORRELATIONS OF TEST V10 (PROOF-READING) WITH:

GRADE	V 1 FIGURES	V 2 DIGITS	V 3 NON-SENSE	V 4 WORDS	V 5 GEOMETRICAL FIGURES	V 6 A's	V 7 K. I.	V 8 2, 3	V 9 RECOGNITION SPELLING	COMPOSITE SPELLING	COMPOSITE READING
III	.21	—.26	.33	.36	.16	—.09	—.33	.04	.80	.38	.73
IV	.20	.24	.20	.60	.22	.36	.32	.23	.30	.29	.40
V	.07	.12	.26	.49	.18	.15	.10	.18	.67	.37	.58
VI	.28	.00	.43	.62	.11	.12	.18	—.14	.38	.48	.33
VII	.07	.32	.54	.68	.25	.23	.19	.24	.49	.41	.30
VIII	.05	.11	.34	.58	.10	.19	.06	.12	.55	.40	.38
MEAN	.15	.09	.35	.56	.17	.16	.09	.11	.53	.39	.45
M. D.	.08	.15	.09	.09	.05	.10	.15	.11	.14	.04	.13

although this coefficient is not reliably greater than that between proof-reading and recognition spelling (0.53). The correlation of proof-reading and the composite of reading (0.45) is only slightly greater than that with spelling (0.39). With the exception of Test V 3 (non-sense) all other variables show low correlations with proof-reading.

The correlations between the various verbal functions have now become so many and complicated that inspection of the arrays of coefficients fails to give as clear an idea of the independent significance of each as is desirable. We need to know more precisely to what extent a function, such as proof-reading, is merely a duplication and to what extent it is independent of other functions. This information will be secured most reliably by computing the partial and multiple correlations in which each variable is given its independent weighting by means of the regression equation.

4. SIMPLE, PARTIAL AND MULTIPLE CORRELATIONS OF SEVERAL VERBAL FUNCTIONS WITH READINGS. The simple correlations given in Table XII are the means of the grade correlations which have been given in Tables V to X. These variables are numbered as follows: (1) composite of reading, (2) recognition spelling, (3) proof-reading, and (4) ability to detect small differences between pairs of words. The entries in Table XII are to be read as follows: r_{12} is the simple correlation between reading and recognition spelling; $r_{12\cdot3}$ is the partial correlation between reading and recognition when the elements common to proof-reading have been eliminated or held constant; $r_{12\cdot34}$ is the partial correlation between reading and recognition when the elements common to both proof-reading and ability to detect small differences have been eliminated or held constant.

The correlations between recognition, proof-reading and ability to detect small differences are fairly high ($r_{23} = 0.53$, $r_{24} = 0.47$, $r_{34} = 0.56$), which means that these variables probably contain a great deal that is common. Each of these variables, however, contains certain factors that are independent of the other two since $r_{23\cdot4} = 0.37$, $r_{24\cdot3} = 0.24$, and $r_{34\cdot2} = 0.42$. Proof-reading contains a great deal that is common to recognition and to ability to detect differences as indicated by the fact that the correlation of the latter two variables drops relatively low when the elements common to the former are eliminated ($r_{24\cdot3} = 0.24$).

TABLE XII

SIMPLE, PARTIAL AND MULTIPLE CORRELATIONS BETWEEN THE VARIABLES
(1) READING, (2) RECOGNITION OF SPELLING, (3) PROOF-READING, AND
(4) ABILITY TO DETECT SMALL DIFFERENCES BETWEEN WORDS

SIMPLE CORRELATIONS	PARTIAL CORRELATIONS FIRST ORDER	PARTIAL CORRELATIONS SECOND ORDER	MULTIPLE CORRELATIONS
$r_{12} = .47$	$r_{12\cdot3} = .31$	$r_{12\cdot34} = .26$	$R_{1\cdot23} = .524$
$r_{13} = .45$	$r_{13\cdot2} = .26$	$r_{13\cdot24} = .19$	$R_{1\cdot234} = .54$
$r_{14} = .39$	$r_{13\cdot4} = .30$	$r_{14\cdot23} = .12$	
$r_{23} = .53$	$r_{14\cdot2} = .22$		
$r_{24} = .47$	$r_{14\cdot3} = .19$		
$r_{34} = .56$	$r_{23\cdot4} = .37$		
	$r_{24\cdot3} = .24$		
	$r_{34\cdot2} = .42$		

Next, consider the correlations of these variables with reading. The simple correlation between reading and recognition ($r_{12} = 0.47$) is almost the same as that between reading and proof-reading ($r_{13} = 0.45$) while that between reading and ability to detect differences is slightly less, ($r_{14} = 0.39$). That these correlations are mainly due to common factors is most clearly indicated by the multiple correlations, which are $R_{1\cdot23} = 0.52$, $R_{1\cdot234} = 0.54$. The latter correlation exceeds the simple $r_{12} = 0.47$ by 0.07. That is to say, when we add to the simple r_{12} the properly weighted contributions of the other two variables which are independent of the elements involved in, or common to the first two variables, the combined correlation is increased from 0.47 to 0.54.

If one is interested in discovering the relative independent, or residual, contributions of the several variables, the facts are given by the partial correlations. For example, the partial correlation $r_{12\cdot34}$ = 0.26, means that the correlation between reading and recognition, which is entirely independent of the correlation due to elements common to recognition, proof-reading, and small difference with reading, is 0.26. [The contribution of proof-reading, independent of recognition and small differences, to the correlation with reading is 0.19, while the correlation of small differences and reading, independent of the elements common to the other two variables, is 0.12. The independent correlations of these variables with reading are small as shown either by the partial correlations or more clearly by the multiple correlations.

The important matter is the appearance of an ability (or abilities) common to reading, recognition spelling, proof-reading, and ability to detect differences between pairs of words which are sufficiently important to produce a substantial correlation between them. That this ability is absolutely essential to good reading is shown by the fact that all of our rapid readers excel in Tests V 4, V 9, and V 10, and that many of our poor readers, in the sense of slow, oral, or silent readers, do poorly in these tests.[4]

From the data thus far presented, we are able to say that some ability, common to these several tests, exists and is one of the essentials of good reading. The data do not enable us to say what the character of the ability is. By hypothesis, this common factor has been defined as *the ability to perceive clearly the characteristic features of words*. In later chapters will be described the results of further investigations for the purpose of analyzing this ability.

5. CORRELATIONS OF THE SEVERAL VERBAL FUNCTIONS WITH SPELLING. Table XIII gives the simple, partial and multiple correlations.

It should be observed that the correlations of recognition spelling and of ability to detect small differences with spelling are larger than were the correlations of these two variables with reading. Proof-reading shows a slightly higher correlation with reading than

TABLE XIII

SIMPLE, PARTIAL AND MULTIPLE CORRELATIONS BETWEEN VARIABLES (1) SPELL-INF, (2) RECOGNITION SPELLING, (3) PROOF-READING, AND (4) ABILITY TO DETECT SMALL DIFFERENCES BETWEEN PAIRS OF WORDS

SIMPLE CORRELATIONS	PARTIAL CORRELATIONS FIRST ORDER	PARTIAL CORRELATIONS SECOND ORDER	MULTIPLE CORRELATIONS
$r_{13} = .63$	$r_{12 \cdot 3} = .54$	$r_{12 \cdot 34} = .50$	$R_{1 \cdot 24} = .63$
$r_{12} = .39$	$r_{12 \cdot 4} = .50$	$r_{13 \cdot 24} = -.08$	$R_{1 \cdot 234} = .63$
$r_{14} = .55$	$r_{13 \cdot 2} = .09$	$r_{14 \cdot 23} = .38$	
$r_{23} = .53$	$r_{13 \cdot 4} = .12$		
$r_{24} = .47$	$r_{14 \cdot 2} = .37$		
$r_{34} = .56$	$r_{14 \cdot 3} = .44$		

[4] Not all of those who do well in these tests are good readers, of course, for there are *other* difficulties which result in poor reading. These will be considered later.

with spelling.   While proof-reading is positively correlated with spelling ($r_{13} = 0.39$) this correlation is wholly due to factors which are identical with those contained in recognition and the ability to detect small differences, since $r_{13 \cdot 24}$ equals approximately zero or actually −0.08.   Properly combining the several variables by the regression equation, yields the significant fact that the multiple correlation with spelling ($R_{1 \cdot 234} = 0.63$) is larger than the multiple correlation with reading ($R_{1 \cdot 234} = 0.54$).

That the abilities to perceive certain essential details of words yield higher correlations with spelling than with reading, leads to these tentative hypotheses.   During reading, the words may be perceived in a way which suffices to call up the meaning but may or may not be perceived with sufficient characteristic detail to reinstate, even partially, the spelling.   That is, it is quite possible that when words are perceived in a certain favorable way during ordinary reading, the bonds involved in spelling the word may be strengthened to some degree.   Certain subjects fail to obtain from words an impression that is adequate for reading, some may secure impressions adequate for reading but not adequate for spelling, others may become not only good readers but also good spellers, through practise obtained by seeing words in a particularly favorable way.

An abundance of evidence from the psychological studies of perception proves that we *learn to see* objects, actions, or words in much the same way that we learn to speak English, play violins or typewrite.   Our habits of perceiving words may be as ineffective as many habits of typewriting, and, being less easy for others to observe, the inappropriate reactions are less likely to be discovered.   Few people would expect a child to discover for himself effective methods of learning to typewrite, and there is less hope that effective methods of perceiving words will be developed without guidance.   That there is a difference in the way good and poor readers (or spellers) perceive words, although these differences do not appear in perception of other materials, is now demonstrated.   The next task is to attempt to analyze and define the perceptual reactions which characterize the good and the poor reader or speller.

D. SUMMARY

1. Tests V 1 to V 8 are useful for detecting defects of vision, of eye-muscle coördination, of speed and accuracy of motor reaction,

and inability to work (attend) persistently. When such defects are suggested, they should be further studied.

2. The correlations between Tests V 1 to V 10 are low except when the materials used are the same or similar. This suggests that there is no "general perceptual ability," but many relatively specific perceptual abilities for specific items—words, digits, letters, etc.

3. Poor performances in Tests V 1 to V 10 are to be explained by one or more such factors as are suggested in (1) above, rather than by defects or deficiencies in "general perceptual ability."

4. Partial and multiple correlations display an ability or abilities, common to all perceptual tests involving words as materials, sufficient to cause fairly high correlations between them. By hypothesis, this common factor is defined as an ability to perceive clearly the significant details of words.

5. The fact that the multiple correlations of these tests with spelling are higher than those with reading suggests the possibility that those subjects who possess *very favorable* form of word perception, are, to some extent, learning (or relearning) to spell during the course of ordinary reading.

CHAPTER VI

AN ANALYSIS OF CERTAIN FUNCTIONS INVOLVED IN ORAL AND SILENT READING

A. DIFFICULTIES ASSOCIATED WITH INAPPROPRIATE FORMS OF PERCEPTION

In the preceding sections, a substantial correlation was found between reading ability and various types of perceptual reactions to words; e.g., the ability to detect small differences between pairs of words; the ability to select a correctly spelled word from a series of incorrect spellings; the ability to proof-read. Studying the relations of these abilities by methods of partial correlation, we found among them certain common abilities which were hypothetically defined as a certain favorable method of word perception. Since many poor readers obtained low scores in these tests, but scores as high as those scores obtained by good readers in similar functions when materials other than words (drawings, digits, etc.) were used, the conclusion was reached that poor reading is not generally due to defective powers of general visual perception. The hypothesis was raised that some learners develop habits of word perception which are favorable to reading, whereas others, for reasons not yet discovered, do not. The latter cases, it was thought, might *be trained* to observe words in an appropriate manner.

In this section will be described further experiments which were conducted for the purpose of providing more intimate acquaintance with the perceptual abilities of good and poor readers, together with a description of certain remedial measures which were adopted.

I. DESCRIPTION OF TESTS V 11 AND V 12

TEST V 11. *Ability to react to an isolated word by correct pronunciation.* This test consisted of a list of 36 words selected from the Ayres-Buckingham Scale on the basis of increasing length and spelling difficulty. The short words include two letters; the longest, thirteen. The subject took a typewritten sheet, pronouncing the words, while the observer recorded the response on another sheet, using symbols to indicate emphases, syllabication, hesitations and any facts observed concerning the method of attack. The score was the number of words correctly pronounced in one of two trials. Following is the list used:

LIST ALPHA

1. me	10. catch	19. marriage	28. arrangement
2. it	11. teach	20. circular	29. information
3. do	12. built	21. estimate	30. magnificent
4. but	13. afraid	22. elaborate	31. acquaintance
5. are	14. travel	23. amusement	32. hippopotamus
6. day	15. prison	24. necessary	33. architecture
7. nine	16. factory	25. difficulty	34. extraordinary
8. card	17. visitor	26. approaches	35. miscellaneous
9. mail	18. measure	27. restaurant	36. conscientious

This test was found to be too easy for readers exceeding the average ability of Grade IV at midyear, but it may be used, of course, on all cases of serious retardation.

TEST V 12. *Ability to react to words in sentences by correct pronunciation—Gray's Oral Reading Test.* Gray's Oral Reading Test consists of 12 paragraphs ranging from very easy to very difficult material and is suitable for use in all grades. This test is given individually.

2. RESULTS OF THE PRONUNCIATION AND ORAL READING TESTS

Table XIV discloses the fact that the ability to pronounce single words is not substantially associated with abilities to "perceive" or "discriminate" such items as drawings, geometrical figures, digits or

TABLE XIV

CORRELATIONS OF THE PRONUNCIATION TEST WITH OTHER VARIABLES. THIRTY SUBJECTS, GRADES III AND IV

TEST V 1 FIGURES	V 2 DIGITS	V 3 NON-SENSE	V 4 WORDS	V 5 FIGURES	V 6 A's	V 7 K. I.
—.15	—.07	.22	.65	.11	—.15	—.14

V 8 DIGITS	V 9 RECOGNITION SPELLING	V 10 PROOF-READING	V 12 GRAY'S ORAL	COMPOSITE READING	ORAL SPELLING	COMPOSITE SPELLING
—.14	.63	.64	.62	.70	.48	.38

letters. Pronunciation is, however, substantially correlated with other abilities in dealing with printed words; the coefficients range from 0.38 to 0.70. From these facts, it may be assumed that the common abilities earlier described are involved in the pronunciation test.

The correlation between the ability to pronounce a series of words and the ability to spell the same series is 0.5. It was, of course, very frequently found that words could be pronounced which could not be spelled. It will be necessary to inquire into the relations of these two functions more carefully in a later section (Chapter VII).

Ability to pronounce words is closely correlated with the various types of perceptual abilities which were found, in Chapter V, to be substantially associated with reading and spelling. Table XIV shows correlations of more than +0.6 with Tests V 4, V 9, V 10, V 12 and the composite of reading.

Table XV gives the correlations of Gray's Oral Reading Test with these variables, for Grades III to VI, separately. The means of the

TABLE XV

CORRELATIONS OF GRAY'S ORAL READING TEST WITH:

GRADE	V 4 WORDS	V 9 RECOGNITION SPELLING	V 10 PROOF- READING	V 10 PRONOUNC- ING WORDS	COMPOSITE SPELLING	COMPOSITE READING
III	.48	.58	.54	.60	.58	.65
IV	.48	.50	.52	.63	.52	.57
V	.42	.47	.46	. . .	.48	.60
VI	.44	.42	.50	. . .	.40	.51
MEAN	.46	.49	.51	.62	.50	.58
M. D.	.02	.05	.02	.02	.06	.04

correlations with the several types of reactions to words are similar to those shown by the pronunciation test. The correlations are not quite so high, chiefly because the coefficients for the pronunciation test were obtained from a group showing a wider range of ability (subjects from Grades III and IV combined).

The correlation of Gray's test with the pronunciation test is 0.62. The former includes certain abilities such as speed of reading which are not measured by the latter. Both provide opportunity to observe the details of the attack upon new and difficult words. The pronunciation test, by extension to include more difficult material, would probably provide the better opportunity for such observation because the experimenter is less encumbered by the necessity of keeping time and because it is less objectionable to call a halt at any moment for repetition of a trial or for other purposes.

3. An Analysis of Errors of Pronunciation

The following is a case typical of many that were encountered. The pupil was doing fair work in Grade VIII except in reading and spelling. The subject's I. Q. on Stanford-Binet was about 125, but achievement in group tests was low, because of slow reading, which averaged a trifle less than one word per second on easy material. Her score in the Gray's Oral Reading Test was exceeded by 90 per cent of our Grade III pupils. She did poorly in all reading tests except the Thorndike-McCall Reading Scale, which measures depth of comprehension rather than rate. She has a wide oral vocabulary but did poorly in visual vocabulary tests because of inability to recognize many of the words. There were no defects of vision, hearing, motor control, "visual imagery," articulation; no general nervousness or, in fact, any organic or physical defects which could be discovered. Her general perceptual abilities, as indicated by tests employing pictures, digits, letters and geometrical figures, were above the median. Her abilities to perceive minute differences in words, to proof-read, to recognize the correct spelling of words were the poorest in her grade group. In fact, the only difficulties found were involved in the perception of *words*.

The following are typical errors of pronunciation: *measure* is pronounced "music"; *circular*, "circle"; *estimate*, "statement"; *arrangement*, "argument"; *conscientious*, "consent"; *acquaintance*, "ac——"; The subject was unable to do more than approximate the first syllables of such words as *hippopotamus, architecture, extraordinary*, although she knew the meaning of all these words when pronounced for her. She required 52 seconds and made 10 errors in reading a passage of 60 words of such difficulty as "The part of farming enjoyed most by a boy is the making of maple sugar." (Gray's Oral Test, passage No. 6.)

Failures in spelling displayed a similar lack of acquaintance with the visual appearance of words, e.g., *afraid* was spelled "farade, afrade, faraid"; *marriage*, "marage, mariage, maraig"; *extraordinary*, "extrodenery, extrary, exterdiny." She could, however, spell word units phonically, for example, *nub, ex, zig, pur.*

The subject appeared always to attempt to deal with the word as a whole in reading or spelling and apparently her acquaintance with word totals was inexact and vague. For example, in the recognition test, the following forms were judged to be correct: *alaborate, necissary, resterant, arrangment.*

Space will not permit the discussion of other individual cases, but the following samples may be considered as typical of reactions frequently found among poor readers. We are not considering here occasional errors due to "lapses" but errors which are persistently made by the subject.

1. Frequent mispronunciation of *familiar words* by responding with a word which is visually similar as a whole or in some detail: *they* is pronounced "the," "these," or "there," etc.; *must*, "most," "much"; *one*, "are"; *me*, "my."

2. Pronunciation of *new or unfamiliar word* as familiar word which looks like it in general or in some detail: *palace* is pronounced "place" or "plate"; *reared*, "read," "ready"; *industrious*, "under"; *dignifying*, "defend," "dinner"; *position*, "postage," *valuable*, "vegetable," *magnificant*, "managed."

3. Correct or nearly correct pronunciation of part of a word followed by a stop, a guess like those in (2) above or by some inarticulate slur: *brilliancy*, "brill-" followed by unwillingness to proceed, embarrassment, etc. Similarly, *industrious*, "indus-," "indoor- no, I can't!" In other cases, the procedure is: *exercises*, "exer," "exit," "excuse," "no!", "ex," etc. In other cases the end of the word is slurred, the subject looking up as if all were well, e.g., *architecture*, "arch-tsch," etc.

4. In continuous reading, in addition to such errors as are described above, occasionally are found the introduction of words suggested by the *context* as well as by the *form* of the words. In the following example, the correct word is given in parentheses: "Once there *was* (lived) a king . . . in the *small* (same) house . . . the *dark* (dull) white masses. The noblest *passions* (possessions) . . . . He spoke at length *courteously* (continuously) *politely* (persistently) and *hesitating* (gratefully)" etc.

It would be interesting to attempt to trace these particular errors as well as others such as omissions, repetitions, etc., to their causes, but it is scarcely essential to our purpose. The'significant facts are (1) the poor readers seem to react to the word vaguely as a whole, or to react chiefly to certain parts of a word (usually the first part) or at least fail to perceive certain significant features of words; and (2) the poor readers usually have no satisfactory method of attacking a new or difficult word. Many of them were quite helpless when they could not recognize the word correctly at a glance. Such inadequacy in the perception of words leads to a variety of undesirable habits which vary with individuals and circumstances. For example: (1) Irregular eye movements, refixations, etc., resulting from the necessity of studying unfamiliar words, or from habits of repeating or skimming the context in order to discover the meaning from words which were familiar; (2) very slow and laborious progress due to prolonged study for purposes of recognition; (3) habits of rapidly guessing at the word as contrasted with (2); (4) narrow eye-voice span, i.e., inability to see ahead of the words being spoken orally or silently; (5) failure to comprehend material because attention is absorbed in the task of recognition or pronunciation; (6) embarrassment, distaste, and other unfavorable emotional reactions of a temporary or permanent character.

Some of the backward readers displaying such difficulties had received very little or no training in perception of words; some had received one or another type of phonetic drill, and others had tried several varieties of such analytical work. The general helplessness of the former and the futility of the efforts of the latter led to the belief that most of the perceptual difficulties were the results of lack of training or inappropriate training, and were to be remedied by systematic practice and instruction.

We have no indubitable evidence that all children are handicapped by lack of specific training in word perception. Most of them do succeed in learning to read by any method of teaching or with no instruction at all. In fact, experts have suggested that the "natural" method, i.e., learning without instruction, is to be desired. That such procedure leads to seriously ineffective habits for a few appeared unquestionable in this study. It is possible that appropriate instruction would have enabled many others to learn more rapidly and with less effort, and to become better readers than would otherwise have been possible.

Not all methods of training in word analysis are effective; at least certain methods do not succeed with all pupils, and some are of doubtful value for all. Our evidence for this belief is the fact that several of our backward readers had been long drilled in certain phonetic methods; in fact, we were led to suspect that such training was occasionally the cause of backwardness. As the "word method" or "natural method" may result in failure to acquire effective methods of perceiving words, certain phonetic, or visual analytical methods may result in inappropriate perception, although the perceptual reactions may be very different in the two cases. Several of our subjects had been given continuous drill in several forms of word analysis without marked improvement of reading. The following is a typical case: I. Q. 116, Grade III, good in arithmetic and writing, poor in spelling and incapable of reading any but simplest prose. There was frequent mispronunciation of easy words "the" for *he*, "mill" for *mail*, etc. When a difficult word was encountered, the subject pronounced a word something like the one observed or proceeded by small phonetic elements, e.g., *afraid*, "a, af-f-f-frr, a-ff-ra," etc. There was a great deal of sounding of individual letters, or of small units without system. For example, in attempting *afraid*, *af*, *fr*, and, *ra*, might each be the unit at different times.

Other types of difficulty to which training in phonetic methods appeared to lead are: (1) Habits of reacting primarily by an effort to pronounce words accurately so that comprehension is inadequate, even in cases where pronunciation is achieved; (2) habits of progressing by very small units, thereby inhibiting development of rate; (3) habits of too explicit articulation, thereby retarding rate; (4) habits of looking directly at words being pronounced, i.e., very narrow eye-voice span.

4. Description of a Method of Training in Word Perception

The determination of effective devices for training in the perception of words is an important problem deserving extensive investigation. The merits of the many phonetic and other analytical methods now in vogue await experimental verification. The usual advice to "use any standard method" betrays the vagueness of our knowledge. There are practically no experimental data concerning any of them, as we discovered during preparations for remedial instruction of such cases as have been described. The procedure devised was the outgrowth of the analytical study of our cases, a

survey of such literature and reading systems as could be found and
some preliminary trial of several methods. That it will need change
and improvement is unquestioned. The following are some of the
criteria upon which the procedure was based:

1. The method should be as simple as possible; one which the
subject could be taught to employ himself. It should not require
the immediate use of books, charts or apparatus, if these can possi-
bly be avoided.

2. The method should be such as not to yield readily to over-use.
Analytical work should not be done for its own sake; no word or practice should be introduced for the sake of the system, a common defect of most phonetic practices.

3. The method should provide against the teaching of what is
already known, what will be known without teaching, or what
ought not to be known. For example, little time should be devoted
to phonetic training for the mass of pupils. The associations between
letter combinations and sounds come, as a rule, without special
effort. The difficulty is not in the *association* between the word and
the sound, but in acquaintance with the *form* of the word. This
distinction is important. Some of our backward cases who were
said to have no "phonic ability," were found to have extraordinary capacity for representing sounds by letters; in fact, they
could give many different combinations of letters which were phonically adequate. That they did not know which one of these the
English race had adopted, was no reflection on their phonic ability.
The futility of much phonetic drill is that the pupils already know
or soon will know without the daily articulatory gymnastics.

More serious is the teaching which establishes habits which are
positively inhibitive of proper development. For example, elaborate drills in pronunciation and word building with such elements as
pl, ch, st, sh, ns, rs, etc., are not only boring and largely futile, but
often the source of real difficulty in word perception, due to the development of habits of attack by such minute elements. For example, note this effort to pronounce service, "see-rrr-seerr-ervy-seer-
see-er"; then, giving this up for a look at the word as a whole the
child shouted, "Oh, *service.*"

4. An acquaintance with many small words as wholes should
precede training in word analysis. What is desired is that the
learner see long words as wholes made up of small words already

known. To have secured a fair visual vocabulary of short words
first is to simplify the whole process and to profit by the greatest
positive transfer.

5. It should be understood that the purpose of analytical work
is not the perception of longer words piece by piece, nor a fund of
information about the composition of words nor a stock of serial reci-
tations such as, "the following words contain ock—sock, flock,
knock, block, crock, etc." What is wanted is the *habit* of seeing a
word as a group of familiar and simpler parts and of seeing it more
clearly, rather than seeing it vaguely or confusedly as one would at
first perceive a complicated Chinese character. Just as the trained
musician hears an orchestra as a whole and at the same time as a
related group of familiar units, whereas the novice hears only a
confusing, undefined storm of noise, so the effective reader sees the
word at once as a whole and as a group of clearly perceptible parts,
whereas certain poor readers see only a confusion of letters. Some
acquaintance with the units, along with practice in appreciating
them in the composite, is essential in either case. What is wanted
is neither an acquaintance with the unanalysed whole nor with the
parts singly, but a clear grasp of a whole of significant parts.

The method adopted comprised two phases: (1) training in observation and analysis of words in the process of learning to spell,
and (2) training in observation and piecemeal attack, when necessary, during the process of reading.

The first method embraced the following features: (1) careful
observation of the printed word during pronunciation by syllables;
(2) attempts to visualize the appearance of the word with eyes
closed during silent articulation by syllables for the purpose of
providing a check on the success of observation; and (3) writing of
the word with silent articulation by syllables. This procedure is
described in detail in the following chapter which deals with spelling. Its purpose is the development of habits of observing words
carefully, together with a method of attack for pronunciation and
spelling.

The perceptual training given during reading instruction involved
briefly the following features. During the oral reading of interesting
material suited to the subject's general mental ability, training in
analysis was given whenever a word was encountered which offered
difficulty. At first the teacher used a card with which she covered

all but the first syllable, asking the pupil to pronounce it. Next the second syllable was exposed alone and pronounced; then the third, etc. Finally the pupil picked out and pronounced the several syllables in succession when the whole word was exposed. Samples of the divisions of words are: vis-i-tor, cir-cu-lar, amuse-ment, ar-range-ment, in-form-a-tion. The procedure was to begin with syllables as the smallest units (unless the pupil did not know the alphabet, which should be taught), and advance to larger units as the pupil was able. The teacher, or better, the pupil himself should learn what units are appropriate at a given stage, and should move on to more inclusive units as progress permits. Pupils must be taught (1) to skip no word of whose pronunciation they are uncertain; (2) to work out the pronunciation whenever possible without assistance; (3) not to sacrifice the meaning in the interest of pronunciation but to reread the sentence as a whole when the delay for analysis has resulted in loss of the thought; (4) to seek for an increase in speed in reading.

5. RESULTS OF TRAINING IN WORD PERCEPTION

Some of the cases of serious backwardness associated with inadequacy in word perception were thus trained in reading and spelling, beginning with easy material and advancing to more difficult. Care was exercised that they should not encounter difficulties so frequently as seriously to endanger fluency and comprehension. These subjects were encouraged to examine isolated words, as circumstances permitted, for the purpose of discovering common units, although this was not done extensively.

Very satisfactory results were obtained; most of these cases improved rapidly in both reading and spelling. Two cases from Grade VIII may be cited as examples:

Case L, Grade VIII, I. Q. 125, obtained a score in Gray's Oral Reading Test which was about the 10 percentile of our Grade III. After six weeks, during which she was given short drills on school days, she obtained a score equal to the median of Grade VII. She was still slow in silent reading but making rapid improvement.

Case Q, Grade VIII, I. Q. 125, who had been a reading and spelling problem for many years, made the equivalent of nearly three years gain, which brought him to the 55 percentile of his grade in less than four weeks of short practice on school days. His speed of silent reading and ability to learn to spell also showed improvement. The period of special training ended with the semester, but the subject, who had previously done practically no reading of his own accord, took a greater interest than usual in general reading during the summer. Tested at the beginning of the school year in November, his rate of reading (Burgess test) was at the 70 percentile score for Grade IX at midyear and his spelling at the 40 percentile for the same grade.

Both forms of training described above were given more or less generally in the several grades, according to individual needs, in addition to training in rapid reading and in comprehension of more conventional types.[1] The improvement achieved by the grades, as wholes, are given the last section of this chapter.

B. A STUDY OF THE DEPTH AND RATE OF COMPREHENSION OF VERBAL MATERIAL

Thus far, interest has centered in the mechanical aspects of reading, but before going further with these considerations, it will be advisable to study the several concepts falling under comprehension, the instruments by which it may be measured, and its relation to other abilities.

1. THE RATE AND DEPTH OF COMPREHENSION OF SENTENCES

It is customary to distinguish two features of comprehension during reading: (1) the power or depth of comprehension and (2) the rate or speed of comprehension. That this distinction is valid has been demonstrated elsewhere,[2] although the tests of the two abilities show, in general, high correlations. In particular cases, however, we have found, in comparison with the mean relation, wide discrepancies which are of utmost importance for diagnostic work. In this investigation, about a dozen representative tests of "rate" and "comprehension" were employed, some of them being repeated, or given in different forms, from 2 to 7 times in order to discover their validity in comparison with a criterion of "rate" and "comprehension," their reliability (consistency), the degree to which they were subject to practice, etc. The tests used are listed in Chap-

[1] For illustrations, see O'Brien, *op. cit.*
[2] "An Experimental and Statistical Study of Reading and Reading ... *Educational Psychology*, Oct., Nov., Dec., 1921.

ter III and the detailed data concerning them will be found in the earlier paper.

It is not necessary to give all these tests for purposes of diagnosis. In fact, the findings indicated that the essential information can be secured by the use of two: (1) Thorndike Reading Scale Alpha 2 or the Thorndike-McCall Reading Scale, which gives the most valid measure of power or depth of comprehension, and (2) the Burgess Picture Supplement Test, the Courtis Test or one of several other tests for "rate" of comprehension. If highly reliable scores are desired, however, it is necessary to give two or more forms of a test.

The mean correlation between the composite of speed tests and the composite of comprehension tests is high, 0.84 ± S. D. 0.08. This figure probably does not represent the real association of *rate* and *depth* of comprehension because it was found that most of the tests which professedly were measures of depth of comprehension were really measures of rate. This fact is suggested by the correlations in Table XVI. The mean correlation of Thorndike-

TABLE XVI

SHOWING THE MEAN OF THE CORRELATIONS FOR THE SEVERAL GRADES, III TO
VIII INCLUSIVE, WITH THE S. D. OF THE SEPARATE GRADE CORRELATIONS
FROM THE MEAN

		BROWN RATE	COURTIS RATE	COURTIS COMPREHENSION	MONROE RATE	MONROE COMPREHENSION	WOODWORTH DIRECTIONS	THORNDIKE-McCALL	MEAN
Thorndike . . .	r	.36	.33	.46	.60	.53	.45	. . .	.46
McCall with . .	S. D.	.14	.23	.15	.16	.14	.25	. . .	.18
Burgess with . .	r	.61	.62	.54	.71	.72	.76	.48	.66*
	S. D.	.12	.14	.18	.07	.08	.11	.17	.12

* Not including r between Burgess and Thorndike-McCall.

McCall with other tests is 0.46 ± S. D. 0.18 as compared with the mean r of 0.66 ± S. D. 0.12 between the Burgess and other tests. The mean of the grade correlations between Burgess and Thorndike-McCall is approximately 0.5, which represents, in our opinion, approximately the actual association of rate and depth of comprehension.

The clearest evidence of the difference in the factors determining success in these tests is obtained by an examination of the scores of children of high I. Q. who were slow readers. Table XVII gives the scores, in terms of percentile ranks, among children of the same grade, for a selection of such cases.

From this table it is clear that the slow readers with superior I. Q.'s have better than average depth or power of comprehension as disclosed by the Thorndike test, but that the percentile scores on all other tests are low. The conclusion is that scores on all tests but Thorndike-McCall are primarily determined by rate rather than by power of comprehension.

TABLE XVII

SHOWING THE SCORES, IN TERMS OF PERCENTILES* FOR THE SUBJECT'S GRADE,
OBTAINED BY BRIGHT PUPILS WHO WERE SLOW READERS

SUBJECT GRADE	THORNDIKE -McCALL	BURGESS P. S. I	MONROE RATE	MONROE COMPRE-HENSION	COURTIS RATE	COURTIS COMPRE-HENSION	BROWN RATE
VIII L.	88	0	0	0	0	0	0
VIII Q	67	6	9	17	15	15	5
VII R	58	38	30	40	20	25	18
VII P	58	44	40	47	32	30	40
VI N	62	26	30	26	22	28	18
V K	55	32	18	20	12	10	6
IV Q	60	30	30	40	28	35	18

* The percentile score is the percentage of cases which the subject in question exceeds in ability.

It should be added that this situation does not obtain among pupils just beginning to read. Certain cases in Grade III, at the beginning of the year, and in Grade II at different stages, were found whose reading was so inadequate that they were unable to do anything with the Thorndike-McCall. Among older cases of backwardness in reading, we have found that a rate of reading as low as one word per second does not seriously handicap the subject for this test, when slowness of reading is the main difficulty. For example, one pupil in Grade VIII who could scarcely read one word per second, obtained a score equal to the norm for Grade XI, which shows that mere slowness of reading need not seriously influence achievement in this test.

2. THE UNDERSTANDING OF ISOLATED PRINTED WORDS

It is possible that poor reading may exist without inadequacy of comprehension of single words. Factors involved in continuous reading, in sentence structure or in dealing with various ideas in contextual association, make provision for considerable specialization. It is therefore important to discover not only the ability to understand sentences but also the ability to comprehend words singly. It will be interesting to compare the poor reader's visual vocabulary with his auditory vocabulary. Two tests of visual vocabulary were used.

A. A special test arranged by the writer. A list of 50 words, ranging from easy to difficult, was taken from the Terman Vocabulary Test, and each word arranged in a series with 5 others of which the one that illustrated the meaning of the original was to be underlined. For example:

    1. gown.......(dress, tree, bird, rain, fish)
    28. bewail.......(sing, praise, lament, curse, invite)
    50. complot.......(fight, conspiracy, lodge, betterment, begging)

The subjects were tested in groups without a time limit.

B. The Holley Sentence Vocabulary Test. At the time preparations were made for this investigation, we were not aware of the existence of Holley's Sentence Vocabulary Scale, which is very similar to the one just described except that 70 words are used, and four instead of five alternatives are offered, for example:

    1. A gown is a ..... string ..... animal ..... dress ..... plant.
    70. Avarice is shown by ..... egotism ..... altruism ..... covetousness ..... melancholy.

This test was subsequently used. The subject works until he has finished. The score is number of correct responses.

A comparison of the scores obtained in the vocabulary tests with those obtained in the Burgess and Thorndike-McCall by the extremely slow readers, shows that the percentile scores for the former fall between the other two. A few samples shown in Table XVIII will suffice for illustration. Difficulties in the mechanics of reading have less effect on the Thorndike-McCall than on the Burgess or the visual vocabulary tests. The very backward readers are, as a rule, conspicuously incapable of handling words visually unfamiliar, so

TABLE XVIII

PERCENTILE SCORES OBTAINED BY VERY SLOW READERS IN:

GRADE SUBJECT	BURGESS	SPECIAL VOCABULARY	THORNDIKE-McCALL	STANFORD I. Q.
VIII L	0	18	88	125
VIII Q	6	28	67	125
V K	32	48	55	106
IV Q	38	48	60	119
III Q	0	10	18	118
III P	26	26	34	95

that in the vocabulary test they frequently fail to recognize words the meanings of which are known; whereas in the Thorndike-McCall they succeed in working out the meaning of a paragraph from those words which are familiar.

Among very backward readers whose deficiencies are not due to any lack of general verbal intelligence, the discrepancies between visual and oral vocabulary are likely to be large. The relations between these two types of verbal abilities will next be considered.

3. THE UNDERSTANDING OF ISOLATED SPOKEN WORDS AND OF SENTENCES

Our data for this function were obtained from the vocabulary test of the Stanford-Binet Tests. One of the two columns of 50 words was used according to the directions for that test while the other column comprised the words used in the writer's visual vocabulary test described above. The results of the two may therefore be directly compared.

Table XIX gives the correlations between these tests for Grades III and IV. The correlation between the two visual vocabulary tests is 0.82 as compared to 0.52, the correlation between the Stanford test and either visual vocabulary test.

That the association between the visual vocabulary tests and reading is higher than the correlation between the Stanford Oral Vocabulary and reading rate is quite clear in these figures: the correlation of Holley with reading rate (Burgess) is 0.63; the author's visual vocabulary with reading rate, 0.67; Stanford Oral with reading rate, 0.20.

TABLE XIX

CORRELATIONS BETWEEN STANFORD ORAL VOCABULARY, THE HOLLEY VISUAL
VOCABULARY, AND THE AUTHOR'S VISUAL VOCABULARY TESTS.
GRADES III AND IV

	STANFORD ORAL	HOLLEY VISUAL	AUTHOR'S VISUAL	BURGESS READING (RATE)	THORNDIKE-MCCALL READING (COMPREHENSION)	COMPOSITE OF SPELLING
Stanford III	...	.42	.45	.10	.59	.49
Oral IV	...	.61	.58	.30	.50	.39
MEAN	...	.52	.52	.20	.55	.44
Holley III	.42	...	.81	.71	.84	.60
Visual IV	.61	...	.83	.55	.58	.37
MEAN	.52	...	.82	.63	.71	.49
Special III	.45	.81	...	.72	.78	.57
Visual IV	.58	.83	...	.62	.51	.40
MEAN	.52	.82	...	.67	.65	.49

The distinction between the relations of the oral and visual vo-
cabulary tests with comprehension is not so great; the correlation of
Stanford Oral with Thorndike Comprehension is 0.55; Holley with
Thorndike, 0.71; and the author's Vocabulary with Thorndike, 0.65.

We have found the Stanford Vocabulary Test to furnish valuable
information not given by other tests, particularly in Grades I, II
and III, and in other cases where reading ability was approximately
zero. In Table XIX it is worthy of notice that whereas in the case
of Grade III, the correlation of the Stanford Vocabulary with rate
of reading is 0.10, the correlation of the visual vocabulary tests
is 0.70. A study of the pupils of this grade disclosed the fact that
many were able to comprehend words given orally but could not
comprehend them in print. We have found it useful to check this
possibility with the oral test in many instances.

Occasionally cases are met displaying average or superior oral
reading ability with surprisingly small power of comprehension in
either oral or silent reading. Such cases represent an over-emphasis
of the articulatory reactions to the exclusion of comprehension, and
when found the Stanford Oral Vocabulary Test is useful in establishing the diagnosis.

It is of course possible that abilities are so specialized that the comprehension of oral sentences might be usefully measured in addition to understanding oral words singly. The score on the Stanford test is fair evidence of this ability, and in cases of doubt the achievement on particular oral problems in that examination were studied.

4. Correlations Between Vocabulary, Reading and Other Tests in the Higher Grades

In order to discover whether the relations between the various vocabulary and reading tests found among pupils just beginning to read are similar to those among pupils whose reading habits are fairly well established, the correlations shown in Table XX were computed.

TABLE XX

Correlations between Variables as Indicated by Headings. $N = 40$
Pupils of Grades VII and VIII

	1 Special Vocabulary	2 Holley Vocabulary	3 Burgess Reading	4 Thorndike-McCall	5 Composite Spelling	6 Detect Difference in Words	7 Proof-Reading
Special Vocabulary	...	.82	.50	.56	.47	.44	.43
Holley Vocabulary	.82	...	.57	.54	.45	.53	.49
Burgess Reading	.50	.57	...	.45	.48	.76	.71
Thorndike-McCall	.56	.54	.45	...	.38	.44	.41
Composite Spelling	.47	.45	.48	.38	...	.73	.54
Detecting Difference in Words	.44	.53	.76	.44	.73	...	.56
Proof-Reading	.43	.49	.71	.41	.54	.56	..

The correlation between the two visual vocabulary tests (0.82) is the same as that found in the lower grades (See Table XIX). The correlations between the visual vocabulary tests and reading are lower in the upper grades; about 0.54 as compared to 0.65 for the Burgess, and 0.46 as compared to 0.68 for the Thorndike-McCall. Correlations of vocabulary tests with spelling are slightly less than 0.5 for both groups.

Correlations of the vocabulary tests with spelling, ability to detect small differences between pairs of words, and proof-reading, are also included in Table XX to show the substantial correlations that obtain between this wide variety of abilities in dealing with verbal material.

5. SUMMARY

The main conclusions from this section are:

1. The Thorndike-McCall Reading Scale measures power of comprehension relatively freed of the mechanical factors involved in reading. Other reading tests (Brown, Burgess, Courtis, Monroe) seem to be measures of *rate* rather than *depth* of comprehension.

2. The correlation between rate and power of comprehension, as represented by the Burgess and Thorndike-McCall tests, respectively, is about 0.5.

3. Where reading ability is nearly zero, the Stanford Oral Vocabulary Test is a valuable supplement to reading tests.

4. Backward readers obtain relatively higher scores in oral vocabulary tests than in visual vocabulary tests.

C. OTHER TYPES OF DIFFICULTY ASSOCIATED WITH BACKWARDNESS IN READING

1. OVER-EMPHASIS OF THE ARTICULATORY RESPONSES

Certain types of formal training result in difficulties in comprehension that are not related to inappropriateness of visual perception of words. Two cases have been encountered. These children, in contrast with many others, could attack and pronounce, at least phonically, words which were far beyond their comprehension. Both ranked high in the various tests for perception of words. Their difficulty was in comprehension. It appeared that for them reading meant chiefly a task of articulation; interpretation being relegated to a curiously subordinate position. If the words were correctly sounded, their feeling was that the task was well done; reading had become a series of exercises in vocal-motor gymnastics.

The remedy here consists in provision of exercises in silent reading to find answers to questions, to carry out directions, to give summaries of paragraphs, etc. In the two cases observed, there was but little difficulty in securing a transition to more appropriate reading habits.

2. INNER SPEECH IN SILENT READING

The association of over-emphasis of oral reading with habits of articulation which may inhibit development of speed in silent reading has been the subject of several studies. Earlier workers have found that habits of responding to printed words by articulating them frequently become so firmly established that they may persist for many years, or even throughout life, in the form of more or less definite lip movement or "inner speech." That "inner speech" might inhibit the development of speed in silent reading, and that a rapid improvement of speed attended training to decrease these motor activities, was demonstrated by Pintner in 1913.[3] These results have been since verified by other investigators.[4]

We observed our subjects for articulation in reading during an individual examination with the Burgess Reading Test. The poorer readers, on the whole, showed lip movement more frequently, but many of the very rapid readers displayed similar habits. There were no cases of serious backwardness among the group, which seemed to be due primarily to vocal-motor habits of these types, unless the cases mentioned in the preceding section are considered as the extremes of this type of difficulty. The attention of the pupil or teacher was called to excessive articulation in silent reading and suggestions for its remedy were given. We were unable to isolate the improvement due to reducing inner speech alone, but other investigations have shown marked increase in speed.

3. INAPPROPRIATE EYE MOVEMENTS

Our interest at this point is in the type of *acquired* habits which operate in reading. A consideration of physical or organic defects of the eyes will be reserved for the last chapter.

Many writers have attributed to the eye-movement habits a leading rôle in the determination of efficiency in reading, as these quotations indicate: "It is in the writer's belief clearly indicated by the above experiments that one of the essentials of natural and rapid reading is that the reader's eye should at once be able to acquire a regular and uniform motor habit of reaction for each line."[5] "The

[3] Pintner, R., "Oral and Silent Reading of Fourth Grade Pupils," *Journal of Educational Psychology*, June 1913.

[4] For a summary, see O'Brien, J. A., *Silent Reading*, Chaps. III and V.

[5] Dearborn, Walter F., *The Psychology of Reading*. Columbia University Contributions to Philosophy and Psychology, 1906, Vol. XIV.

difference in reading rate is largely a matter of the rhythmical motor habits into which the eye is trained in early attempts to read." [6] "Regular rhythmic movements of the eye are prerequisite to rapid silent reading." [7]

It appears to be the belief of these and other writers that some learners acquire inappropriate motor habits which become so fixed as to inhibit progress. While the literature does show irregular and doubtless inappropriate eye movements to be associated with poor reading almost invariably, it does not show that the inappropriate eye movements are the *cause* of poor reading. The evidence that they are the *result* of poor reading is more weighty. They are a necessary symptom of poor reading but other symptoms are easier to secure. When a pupil reads Gray's oral passages with repetitions, omissions, etc., we may safely assume that the eye movements are inappropriate. The causes of these symptoms are various. Defects of vision of eye-muscle control, too explicit articulation, inappropriate habits of word perception and other difficulties may be at the bottom of the trouble which is remedied by removing the more fundamental cause. The eye movements usually conform readily to new demands; in fact, they seem to do so with very great facility.

Eye movements can be recorded perfectly only by means of elaborate photographic or other graphic methods. [8] Such apparatus was not available for our work, but we undertook a course of training in the direct observation of eye movements while the subject read some appropriate material such as Gray's Silent Reading Test passages. One shortly develops sufficient skill to count the number of fixation pauses and to detect refixation movements with accuracy satisfactory for purposes such as ours. A study was made of about fifteen cases before, during, and after several types of practice.

No cases were found among our subjects in which any form of inappropriate eye movements seemed to be the cause of serious back-

[6] Fordyce, Charles, "Testing the Efficiency in Reading," *Addresses and Proceedings of the N. E. A.*, 1917, Vol. 55, p. 821.

[7] Gray, W. S., "Principles of Method in Teaching Reading as Derived from Scientific Investigation," *Eighteenth Yearbook of the National Society for the Study of Education*, 1919, Part II, p. 40.

[8] For a description of such methods see Gray, C. T., *Types of Reading Ability Exhibited Through Tests and Laboratory Exercises*. Supplementary Educational Monograph, No. 5. Chicago: Univ. of Chicago Press, 1917.

wardness or disability. The movements were very changeable and readily improved as the result of other forms of training. Furthermore, efforts to improve reading by direct training in eye movements were futile. The direct training, consisting of looking across lines with fixation points indicated by dots or words, reading easy material with colored marks indicating fixation points, and some work with gradually increasing perceptual units printed in columns in ordinary type failed to produce any perceptible improvement among the few seriously retarded cases that were tried. This was not refined work, and the number of cases was small. It was our conviction, however, that we were not getting at the seat of the trouble by investigating the eye movements in these subjects.

While it is our belief that inappropriate eye movements, except those caused by defective eye muscles, are never the cause of serious disability in reading, it is probably true that among normal readers habits of comfortable mediocrity are frequently formed, which set a limitation to the speed of reading. Adults often find that they can break up these habits by deliberately pushing ahead to greater speed of eye progress, sometimes voluntarily adopting a rapid rhythm of wide spans, to which comprehension often becomes adapted. The facts of "skimming" portray a considerable amount of voluntary control of these functions.[9] This is, however, quite a different matter from the consideration of inappropriate eye movements as a primary cause of disability in reading.

4. NARROWNESS OF THE EYE-VOICE SPAN

Buswell has made a thorough-going analysis of the relationship between perception and vocal response in reading which is termed the "eye-voice span."[10] It is found that a wide and flexible span, i.e., ability to look ahead of the word being pronounced, is characteristic of good oral and silent reading. In the original investigation Buswell employed eye photographic apparatus which was synchronized with a dictaphone. He has devised a simpler test consisting of a passage which contains such words as *tears*, *read*, *minute*, *does*, that are pronounced differently according to the subsequent context. The

[9] Whipple, G. M. and Curtis, J. N., "Preliminary Investigation of Skimming in Reading." *Journal of Educational Psychology*, June 1917.
[10] Buswell, G. T., *An Experimental Study of the Eye-Voice Span in Reading.* Supplementary Educational Monographs, No. 17, 1920.

reader with a narrow eye-voice span makes a larger number of erroneous pronunciations.

The latter test, which was employed in certain cases, was found to be a useful supplement to Gray's Oral and the Pronunciation test. The backward readers appeared to have narrower spans, as a rule, but this fact, like that of irregular eye movements, is not sufficient for diagnosis. The causes lie deeper, and when they are removed the eye-voice span will broaden; at least, this is what occurred in the cases under our observation.

Further consideration of the causes of backwardness in reading will be reserved for the last chapter. Our purpose here, primarily, is to describe the form of the difficulties found. The association of causes of difficulty in reading and spelling is close. Poor readers are very frequently poor spellers, although many poor spellers are found among average or superior readers. Several features of backwardness in spelling will further an understanding of the nature of backwardness in reading. These will be taken up in Chapter VI.

D. IMPROVEMENT IN READING ABILITY AS THE RESULT OF INSTRUCTION DURING THE YEAR

1. GROSS IMPROVEMENT BY GRADES

Training in visual perception and analysis, as described in Section A of this chapter, was used to some extent, and the method of word study employed in learning spelling, described in the next chapter, was introduced more extensively in the grades. Several devices for the encouragement of rate and comprehension, such as reading paragraphs for the purpose of writing or reciting summaries, to find answers to questions, to carry out instructions, etc., were at times employed. In individual cases, attention was given to excessive articulation, inadequate comprehension, and other difficulties according to the need. As a result, the improvement secured may not be attributed to any one cause, but to the composite of general practices and individual treatments.

Table XXI shows the improvement of the several grades in comprehension, measured by the Thorndike-McCall, and in rate, measured by a composite of the Courtis, Monroe, and Brown tests. The raw scores for the several tests were converted into grade positions, and Table XXI gives the median of the group. Thus 3.0 means beginning of Grade III; 3.5 means Grade III at mid-year, etc.

TABLE XXI

IMPROVEMENT IN RATE AND COMPREHENSION OF READING
Figures indicate Grade Norms attained at stated times
COMPREHENSION (THORNDIKE-MCCALL)   RATE (COURTIS, MONROE, BROWN)

GRADE	NOV.	JAN.	MAY	IMPROVEMENT GRADE YEARS	NOV.	JAN.	MAY	IMPROVEMENT
III	2.8	3.7	4.1	1.3	2.5	3.1	4.7	2.2
IV	4.5	5.3	6.2	1.7	3.7	4.5	6.1	2.4
V	5.8	6.4	7.0	1.2	4.7	6.0	7.2	2.5
VI	6.6	7.2	8.0	1.4	5.8	7.2	9.8	4.0
VII	8.1	8.3	9.2	1.1	7.0	9.0	10.0 + *	3.0 +
VIII	8.2	8.4	10.5	2.3	8.2	9.0	10.0 + *	1.9 +
MEAN				1.5				2.7 +

* Scores were above the estimated grade 10 norms.

The improvement in Thorndike-McCall averages 1.5 years. On the basis of I. Q., we should expect an improvement of 1.17 years. In an earlier section of this study evidence was given that the Thorndike-McCall does not yield rapidly increasing scores as the result of improvement in the mechanics of reading, nor (as indicated in another paper) [11] does this ability increase much as a result of specific training. Improvement in it seems to be primarily determined by growth of general mental ability or by the increase of general information or by both.

The improvement-in-rate averages are considerably more than 2.7 years, actually, because Grades VII and VIII included many subjects who went far above the highest norms. Many completed certain tests, particularly the Monroe, without error in less than the time limit, so that their abilities were not adequately measured. At the end of the year, all grades were well above the norms in both speed and comprehension.

2. CORRELATIONS OF INITIAL ABILITY WITH FINAL ABILITY AND
    WITH AMOUNT OF IMPROVEMENT

Rate of reading was measured by a composite of tests given in November, and again in May; amount of improvement was the

[11] Gates, A. I., "An Experimental and Statistical Study of Reading and Reading Tests," *Journal of Educational Psychology*, Oct. 1921.

TABLE XXII

CORRELATIONS FOR RATE OF READING (1) BETWEEN INITIAL AND FINAL STATUS, AND (2) BETWEEN INITIAL STATUS AND IMPROVEMENT

GRADE	1 INITIAL AND FINAL STATUS	2 INITIAL STATUS AND IMPROVEMENT
III	.79	—.03
IV	.59	—.48
V	.44	—.50
VI	.91	+.07
VII	.82	—.16
VIII	.84	—.24
MEAN	.73	—.22
M. D.	.15	.18

difference between the two scores. Table XXII gives the correlations.

The correlations between initial and final abilities range from 0.44 to 0.91, average 0.73. Considering the range of abilities in these grades, the implication is that despite special attention to the backward individuals during the year, the relative abilities of the pupils were not greatly changed. All improved, some a great deal, but the initially superior maintained, with few exceptions, their superiority in rank.

The correlations between initial scores and the gross improvement during the year vary considerably, but the average result is a negative coefficient, −0.22. That is,,generally speaking, the very backward pupils made a greater gain in terms of gross score than the initially superior. These correlations should not be interpreted to mean that the poorer readers in general improve more rapidly than the better ones, but that they were making progress where it is more readily made, i.e., nearer the beginning of a parabolic learning curve. The correlations are more emphatically negative than they ordinarily would be, partly because the backward cases secured more practice, and partly because of the special attention to the correction of their inhibitive defects.

Table XXIII gives the results for *comprehension* in reading, as measured in November and May by the Thorndike-McCall test. Considering the fact that the range of abilities in the groups as

TABLE XXIII

CORRELATIONS FOR COMPREHENSION (THORNDIKE-MCCALL) (1) BETWEEN
INITIAL AND FINAL STATUS, AND (2) BETWEEN INITIAL STATUS AND
IMPROVEMENT

GRADE	1 INITIAL AND FINAL STATUS	2 INITIAL STATUS AND IMPROVEMENT
III	.66	—.50
IV	.48	—.27
V	.61	+.13
VI	.56	—.10
VII	.48	+.10
VIII	.44	+.06
MEAN	.54	—.10
M. D.	.07	.19

shown by this test is not great, and that, for the particular individual, some forms are easier than others, the correlation of 0.54 between initial and final ability indicates a close relationship. Correlations of initial capacity with improvement are practically zero, excluding Grade III. The correlation of —0.50 for that group is due to the fact that several backward cases were unable to read the material at all in November, whereas the acquisition of only slight reading ability would have enabled them to earn a fair score.

While the attention to defects and difficulties, together with the remedial measures adopted, produced great improvement among the backward cases, very few were able to match the achievements of their initially superior companions, and in all likelihood very few ever will.

E. SUMMARY

A. Difficulties Associated with Inappropriate Forms of Perception.

1. Correlations show that word-perception is an important determinant of success in the pronunciation of words and in oral reading.

2. Characteristic errors of pronunciation result from the perception of words rather vaguely as wholes, the perception of certain portions only, or various other inappropriate perceptual habits.

3. Lack of training in word-perception, inappropriate phonetic or other analytical training and other positive factors are generally responsible for inadequate forms of word perception.

4. A method of training in word-perception, comprising the following features, was adopted: (1) words mispronounced in reading were studied in piecemeal by (2) division into syllables exposed singly with effort to increase gradually the size of the unit to two or more syllables, followed by (3) re-reading of sentence or paragraph to keep comprehension foremost.

B. The Depth and Rate of Comprehension.

1. While depth and rate of comprehension are substantially correlated, pupils whose reading is very slow, due to mechanical difficulties, may achieve high comprehension scores on the Thorndike-McCall Reading Scale.

2. It appears that all other reading tests, given according to standard directions, measure rate, primarily, rather than depth of comprehension.

3. Visual vocabulary tests are inadequate measures of general verbal ability in the case of poor readers. The Stanford Oral Vocabulary Test is a useful instrument in such cases.

C. Other Types of Difficulty in Reading.

1. Occasional cases are found who have greatly emphasized the mechanics of reading to the neglect of comprehension, i.e., they can recognize and pronounce words well but fail to comprehend.

2. Too precise silent articulation or "inner speech" may retard development of speech in reading, although it probably never causes serious incapacity in reading, except as indicated in (1).

3. Inappropriate eye-movements (acquired) and narrowness of the eye-voice span are the almost invariable accompaniments of poor reading but seldom, if ever, the cause of it.

D. Improvement in Reading Ability.

1. Various types of training devised to meet individual needs resulted in very great improvement in the rate of reading,

and in more than average, but less marked improvement in comprehension.

2. Although the correlation between initial ability and gross amount of improvement is negative, the initially superior readers, generally speaking, maintain their relative advantages after practice.

CHAPTER VII

AN ANALYSIS OF ABILITIES INVOLVED IN SPELLING

The close association of spelling with the several functions in which words were used as materials, has constantly been noted. The multiple correlation of ability to detect small differences in words, to recognize the correct form of words, and to proof-read with spelling was found earlier in this study to be higher (0.69) than the multiple correlation of these functions with reading (0.54). Rate of silent reading, oral reading and pronunciation of words are likewise substantially correlated with spelling. The problem of this chapter is to inquire more deeply into the significance of these relations and to study certain additional functions which are involved in successful spelling.

A. THE INFLUENCE OF THE TYPE OF WORD PERCEPTION
UPON SPELLING

TEST 22. *Ability to react to a spoken word by saying its letters (oral spelling).* This test was given individually immediately following the pronunciation test. The same words were used. In each case we began with the easiest words, going through the entire list or at least well beyond the subject's ability. After a short interval, the same list was again spelled orally. Records were kept of all errors, divisions, emphases, etc.

TEST 23. *Ability to react to a spoken word by written spelling.* Following the oral spelling, the subject wrote the same words as they were pronounced by the experimenter. Great care was exercised to prevent the subject from discovering whether his spellings were correct or incorrect. Completing the series, the subject was given a new sheet of paper on which the spellings were written for a second time and in some cases for a third time.

From the material collected, a mass of information concerning the types of errors made, the probable source of errors, their consistency, their relation to the form of reaction to mispronunciation of words, etc., has been collected; but only the data which bear directly on the diagnostic value of the tests will be presented here.

Table XXIV is based upon the records of 30 subjects, most of whom are from Grades III and IV. It gives the correlations of the oral spelling test with other variables.

Close correlations are found between oral spelling and other types of reactions to words. The correlations with recognition spelling, pronunciation, Gray's oral reading, the composite of reading and the ability to detect small differences in words are substantially

TABLE XXIV

CORRELATIONS OF ORAL SPELLING TEST (36 WORDS) WITH OTHER VARIABLES.
DATA BASED ON 30 PUPILS OF GRADES III AND IV

V 1 FIGURES	V 2 DIGITS	V 3 NON-SENSE	V 4 WORDS	V 5 GEOM. FIGURES	V 6 A's	V 7 K. I.	V DIGITS
—.20	.09	.21	.50	.14	—.07	—.17	—.16

V 9 RECOG. SPELLING	V 10 PROOF-READING	PRO-NUNCIA-TION	WRITING SPELLING	COMP. SPELLING	GRAY'S ORAL	COMP READING	
.61	.44	.48	.87	.82	.60	.44	

positive, whereas the correlations with non-verbal functions are near zero. From these data, fresh evidence is gathered in support of the hypothesis that the type of word perception which is favorable to reading is favorable, if not essential, to the development of effective spelling ability.

The oral spelling tests enabled us to secure some information concerning the methods of dealing with words by which the poor spellers differed from the able. By describing certain typical cases in some detail, a clue to the methods of perceiving and spelling words which seem to be unfavorable may be secured.

The following case illustrates ineffective habits of word perception which have occasioned backwardness in both reading and spelling.

This subject was in Grade III, I. Q. 116. He was a very poor oral reader, barely able to read the simplest passage in Gray's Oral Reading Test. His depth of comprehension (Thorndike-McCall) was about the 40 percentile for his class; speed of silent reading, 10 percentile; visual vocabulary, 25 percentile; oral vocabulary, 50 percentile; spelling ability, 10 percentile. He appeared to have no visual, auditory or motor defects. His ability in "general visual perception" as indicated by the tests with drawings, geometrical figures, digits, letters, etc., was about average. His ability to perceive small differences in words was low, 10 percentile. He was a very poor proof-reader and his recognition spelling was the poorest in the class.

There appeared to be no inability to translate short phonic ele-✓ ments into letters; i.e., *in, up, tid, non*, etc., could be spelled. Short words on which he had practiced were correctly spelled, e.g., *me, but, are, day*. He failed on most words containing four letters, and on nearly all longer words. When new or long words were given, he frequently spelled the first syllable, but went astray on others, or spelled, with few letters, a word which sounded more or less like the proper word or resorted to a futile phonetic procedure, for example: *nine*, "nin," "nen," "nu-ni, n-n," etc.; *mail*, "mal," "mill," "ma-ma, m-mal;" *travel*, "tr-tr-a-av."

In pronunciation, the procedure was similar: *card*, "ca - cah - ca - ("oh") - card"; *factory*, "ff - a - a - fac - f-f-fak - factr - ff - a - tr, fac- tor"; *visitor*, "vizzer," "fist," v - v - eye - tt," etc.

In oral reading this subject appeared to perceive words in some way which was not effective for ready recognition. If his first effort to pronounce was incorrect, he resorted to a narrow analytical method in which the single letters, or phonetic elements *is, th, et*, etc., were units. There was much repetition of buzzings, hissings, and sputtering over the small units with very infrequent success during oral reading.

He was unable to recognize many words which he could not spell; in fact, in our tests the number of recognitions and spellings were the same. He performed the recognition test by spelling the word, accepting the form which agreed with the spelling instead of rec- ognizing the word by direct observation. Such words as were con- sistently spelled, it appeared, were learned by direct practice in the motor responses of the letter series. He was at a great disadvantage compared with others who probably relearned the spellings, at least in part, during ordinary reading.

A change in the form of work with words, in which syllables became the units of attack rather than the word as a whole, the letters or the phonetic elements, resulted in rapid improvement.

Space will not permit the discussion of the details of other cases; but in the following paragraphs will be given examples of several typical forms of ineffective methods of attack in spelling.

1. *Spelling letter by letter.* In such case it appeared that no technique of learning had been employed—mere motorization without helpful emphasis, syllabication or division of any kind. This was very frequently found.

2. *Spelling by phonetic units.* The child's attention seemed to center on minute phonetic elements such as *sh, ch, ie, ns,* etc. Unless we are seriously mistaken, this type of training is futile, and sometimes positively inhibitive to success in either spelling or reading.

3. *Unsystematic divisions into various word units,* e.g., *visitor,* "vi-es-tor," "vis-ter," "v-ist-er," "vist-or"; *amusement,* "a-mus-ment," "amus-ment," "am-us-tent." This type of attack indicates lack of uniformity or system in perception and in the initial practice in spelling.

4. *Spelling words by wholes.* In many cases the spelling was correctly and often rapidly made in the case of familiar words, or in the case of short words. Usually the successful spelling came to an abrupt halt when a new word or one exceeding a particular length was encountered. The subject then often failed altogether, said "I can't"; made futile efforts, or spelled the initial portion, then halted or guessed wildly. For example: *measure,* "meas—" or "meas —r"; *circular,* "cirrian," "cirl," "cur—"; *estimate,* "est—," "est-ment"; *difficulty,* "defit." Sometimes the word as a whole set up the spelling of some other word more or less similar phonically. These were not cases of misunderstanding, since the child pronounced them after hearing them. For example: *necessary,* "nursery"; *difficulty,* "differ"; *prison,* "person," "present."

5. *Miscellaneous.* There were, of course, myriads of errors due to lapses, habitual mispronunciations, transfers of "sets" or "tendencies" set up by other words, and others due to peculiarities in the sound-letter relations, so common in English, which were of minor importance for purposes of diagnosis.

Our interest centered chiefly on the attack which the subject made. It is probable that the type of attack indicated the way in which the words were observed. If they were observed as wholes, the spelling was usually correct up to a certain length beyond which the pupil was unable to proceed effectively. He might try to spell letter by letter, or approximate the whole, or try it by parts, now one way now another, but unless the significant details of the word had been observed specifically, a correct spelling would seldom result. In other cases the single letters, or phonetic elements, or incidental features of words might be the center of attack. What was needed was a method of observing a word as a group of parts, each of which is not too minute and not too complex to handle, and which enables him to perceive the significant portions clearly. Many of our backward cases were unable to do this, with the result that they often failed to read and more frequently failed to spell the long or unfamiliar words.

These results confirm the findings of the previous chapter, dealing with reading, to the effect that an inappropriate method of observing words is the common associate of backwardness. The correlation between reading and spelling has been found continually to be high. Backwardness in reading has been, among our subjects, almost invariably accompanied by backwardness in spelling, although backwardness in spelling is not always evidence of backwardness in reading. When the perceptual abilities are so inappropriate as to make reading difficult, other things being normal, the effect on spelling is very marked. When the perceptual abilities are satisfactory for reading they may still be insufficiently precise for perceptible assistance in spelling. Finally, cases of backwardness in spelling are found where the perceptual reactions to words seem better than average. It will therefore be necessary to study several other types of activities involved in spelling.

B. A COMPARISON OF RECOGNITION WITH RECALL OF THE SPELLING OF WORDS

It will be recalled that the test of recognition (Test V 9), described in Chapter V, contained the same thirty-six words used in the pronunciation and in the oral and written spelling tests. Ten or fifteen minutes after these tests—the subject having taken Gray's Oral Reading Test in the interim—the Recognition Test was given, without time limit. Since it was found to be instructive in many cases to compare the achievement in spelling (recall) with the recognition of the correct spellings, some of the pertinent facts will be summarized:

TABLE XXV

AVERAGE NUMBER OF WORDS RECOGNIZED, SPELLED ORALLY, AND SPELLED
BY WRITING. TOTAL NUMBER OF WORDS 36

GRADE	WORDS RECOGNIZED	RECALL ORALLY	RECALL WRITTEN
III	19.0	12.0	12.8
IV	26.0	17.6	18.1
V	30.9	22.5	24.2
VI	31.9	24.6	26.4
VII	32.0	25.7	28.0
VIII	34.6	26.1	28.2
MEAN	29.1	21.4	23.0
M. D.	4.4	4.4	5.0

1. The correlation between ability to recognize the correct spelling of a word and ability to recall it (oral spelling) is 0.63, when the same words are used for both tests. The correlation between Recognition and the Composite of Spelling is 0.60 (see Table XXIV).

2. The spelling of a word can often be recognized when it cannot be recalled, as shown in Table XXV. The average results are: out of a possible 36 words, 29 are recognized; 23 correctly spelled in writing; and 21.4 spelled orally.

It is well known as the result of many studies [1] that the subject may often recognize items which he cannot recall. The case mentioned earlier, in which recall and recognition of the words were equal, is exceptional. It is to be expected on general principles that recognition will exceed recall, where the same words are involved.

Table XXVI gives the distribution of 100 cases according to the number of words by which the recognitions exceeded recall, the latter being measured by oral spelling. Four cases, showing a difference of 0 or 1, constitute one end of a fairly regular probability distribution; four cases, showing a difference of 14 to 16, the other. The median difference is about 8 words. (See Table XXV for average gross differences in comparison with gross number recognized and recalled.)

3. The difference between the number of words recognized and the number recalled varies considerably among different individuals,

[1] See, for example, E. Mulhall Achilles, *Experimental Studies in Recall and Recognition*. Archives of Psychology, No. 44, 1920.

TABLE XXVI

NUMBER OF WORDS BY WHICH RECOGNITION EXCEEDS RECALL
(ORAL SPELLING)

NUMBER RECOGNIZED MINUS NUMBER RECALLED	NUMBER OF CASES
0–1	4
2– 3	10
4– 5	14
6– 7	19
8– 9	26
10–11	15
12–13	8
14–15	3
16	1
Total	100

and is frequently as great among poor spellers as among good spellers. In fact, the correlation between oral spelling and the difference (i.e., number recognized minus number spelled) is +0.08 for a sample group (Grade III). Table XXVII, which gives the scores for groups of good and poor spellers of Grades III and IV, shows the situation more concretely. The good spellers recognize a considerably larger number of words—the correlation for these two abilities in the different grades averages 0.63 (see page 70)—but the discrepancies between recall and recognition show a great range for good and poor spellers alike.

A careful study of all available data concerning many of these cases, especially those at the extremes, has led to certain hypotheses concerning the relations of these two functions.

The first is that for effective spelling, the bonds between the perception (visual or auditory) of the word and the motor reactions of producing the letters in serial order must in the first place be established by specific practice. That is, no matter how helpful a favorable type of word perception may be, it is not sufficient in and of itself to establish correct recall of the exact spelling. Those cases which show a great superiority of recognition over recall are to be explained by failure to learn the spellings of words in the first place. For this, three explanations are offered: 1. Inertia, lack of interest or lack of motivation in the particular kind of learning involved in spelling. 2. Ineffective methods of practice in forming these

TABLE XXVII

NUMBER OF WORDS RECOGNIZED, NUMBER CORRECTLY SPELLED ORALLY, AND
DIFFERENCE BETWEEN THE TWO, FOR GROUPS OF GOOD AND POOR
SPELLERS, GRADES III AND IV

GOOD SPELLERS

GRADE III			GRADE IV		
1 WORDS RECOGNIZED	2 WORDS SPELLED	3 DIFFERENCE	1 WORDS RECOGNIZED	2 WORDS SPELLED	3 DIFFERENCE
29	22	7	31	24	7
30	22	8	30	21	9
17	15	2	30	20	10
26	15	11	24	20	4
Mean 25.5	18.5	7.0	29.0	21.0	7.5

POOR SPELLERS

GRADE III			GRADE IV		
7	7	0	25	12	13
18	8	10	22	14	8
25	9	16	24	15	9
15	9	6	27	15	12
Mean 16.0	8.0	8.0	24.5	14.0	10.5

specific bonds. 3. Inability to form these bonds readily as a result
of endowment (disability).

That lack of interest or application is frequently responsible for
the lag of real achievement in spelling behind possible achievement,
cannot be doubted. While the causes of the lack of interest or application are probably many, it is quite likely that ineffective methods
of learning to spell are among them. That many of the pupils studied in this investigation had failed to develop effective methods of
spelling has been indicated. The improvement of spelling achievement in Grades III to VI inclusive as the result of the introduction
of a method of spelling which was in operation during about three-
fourths of the year, may be considered as evidence on these points.
The data are given in Table XXX. With the exception of one sub-

ject, marked improvement in spelling ability was achieved. While individual differences in native aptitude for learning to spell undoubtedly exist, the extreme backwardness found was due primarily to inadequacy of motivation or methods of learning. These matters will be treated in greater detail in the next section of this chapter and again in Chapter VIII.

Our second general hypothesis may now be repeated. When once the specific reactions which constitute the spelling of a word have been established, a certain "favorable" type of perception in reading does, to some extent, exercise and thus preserve these reactions. The evidence for this hypothesis is, to be sure, indirect. Briefly it is as follows: (1) The better readers are, in general, better spellers; (2) the better readers and spellers show, in general, greater ability to detect small differences between words; (3) the better readers and spellers excel in recognition of the correct spelling of words and in proof-reading; (4) where recognition spelling greatly exceeds recall spelling, the difficulty is to be found in lack of effort, of method, or of specific ability to form the specific reactions required for actual spelling. That is, taking all evidence into account, it appears that the method of perceiving words, characteristic of the good reader, is of material assistance in preserving the bonds which are essential to successful spelling.

The types of perceptual attack in learning to spell which are unfavorable have already been suggested. One other consideration remains, namely, the question of the type of motor expression which is most desirable for spelling.

C. THE RELATION OF SPELLING TO THE FORM OF REACTION BY WHICH IT IS EXPRESSED

I. GENERAL CONSIDERATIONS

The spelling of a word may be learned by practice of several different reactions: Writing; articulation, silent or aloud; "visualization"; typewriting, and doubtless in many other ways. On general principles, we would predict that the word will be most surely and accurately spelled, on demand, in the way in which it has been most thoroughly practiced. Usually the subject can spell the word in more than one way, but usually one way is superior to others; and occasionally we find that a word can be written but not spelled orally or "visualized," at least not until the writing reaction has been consummated. If practice in spelling were predominantly "visualization" or articulation, we would expect to find cases in which the subject could not write the word, at least not without using one of the former reactions as a means of attaining the latter.

Table XXVIII gives the relative success of written spelling as compared to oral spelling for 100 cases, arranged by grades. In general, written spelling excels, the superiority becoming more marked

TABLE XXVIII

NUMBER OF WORDS BY WHICH WRITTEN SPELLING EXCEEDED ORAL SPELLING
100 CASES

Number Written Minus Oral	GRADES					
	III	IV	V	VI	VII + VIII	TOTAL
—6	..	1	..	..	..	1
—5	..	..	..	..	..	0
—4	..	..	..	..	..	0
—3	1	1	..	..	..	2
—2	1	1	..	1	..	3
—1	2	2	1	3	2	10
0	8	3	6	1	..	18
+1	4	4	1	7	3	19
2	1	4	3	4	4	16
3	2	1	3	2	4	12
4	..	1	3	1	3	8
5	..	..	1	..	2	3
6	1	1	1	2	1	6
7	..	..	..	1	1	2
Mean No. of Cases	0.55	1.63	2.0	2.0	2.8	1.56
	20	19	19	22	20	100

as the grade becomes higher. We have no reason to believe that these facts imply that original nature is such that letter combinations can be acquired through finger movements more readily than through oral movements, or vice versa in the exceptional cases. The facts are more probably accounted for by the predominance of practice by means of writing, which becomes greater in the upper grades. The prime need for spelling ability is to make legible writing possible, and it is during writing that most of the specific practice in spelling is obtained.

Since the motor mechanisms of articulation and writing are directly concerned in spelling, it is possible that ineffective control of these mechanisms may contribute to poor spelling. It is important to consider both of these possibilities in diagnostic work, particularly if the difference between oral and written spelling is marked.

2. POOR SPELLING ASSOCIATED WITH POOR WRITING ABILITY

The one case in which oral spelling was markedly superior to written appeared to be associated with poor penmanship and a generally inferior motor coördination of fingers and hand. There was no evidence that this case represents a constitutional difficulty in forming mental connection between sounds and writing reactions: The more probable explanation is that because of difficulty in writing, the subject practiced spelling by articulation with the result that the former connections were less adequately formed. The spelling ability of this subject was considerably below the mean for his age and grade, due largely to lack of practice in writing words.

Two other cases showing a less marked superiority of oral over written spelling were marked by a poor quality and careless method of writing, while other cases seemed to be due entirely to a predominance of oral spelling practice. All of these cases were backward but not the poorest in their grades in general spelling ability. Inferior writing ability was doubtless partly responsible for their backwardness.

Since the association of poor spelling with poor writing has been observed by other workers, some attention was given to this relation among our subjects. Table XXIX gives the correlation of writing ability (the score was the product of quality on the Thorndike Scale by number of letters written per minute) with spelling ability and with reading ability.

The correlations of writing with spelling average 0.18 but show a more uniform positive relation than do the correlations between reading and writing, which average 0.12. In neither case is the association of any clear significance. In this, as with other functions, the correlation may conceal important facts because only extremely poor writing is causally related to spelling efficiency.

TABLE XXIX

CORRELATIONS OF WRITING WITH COMPOSITE OF SPELLING AND WITH
COMPOSITE OF RATE OF READING

GRADE	WRITING WITH SPELLING	WRITING WITH READING
III	.28	.31
IV	.39	.54
V	.13	—.46
VI	.15	.00
VII	.12	.16
VIII	.00	.19
MEAN	.18	.12
M. D.	.11	.24

An examination of the records of poor readers and spellers shows good, bad, and average writing. In a number of cases we have been led to suspect that both poor spelling and writing were due either to general indifference toward these subjects or to lack of proper training in them. Carelessness in writing would, of course, be unfavorable to accurate spelling. Laborious and illegible writing, whether due to native inaptitude or to poor training, would place a serious inhibition on one important form of spelling practice, so that when poor writing is found it should be improved, if possible, in the interest of spelling if not for its own sake.

3. THE INFLUENCE OF SPEECH DEFECTS

Speech defects were noted particularly in the Pronunciation test, in Gray's Oral Reading Test, and in incidental conversation. Certain subjects were referred to specialists for examination. What seemed to be rather clear evidence of inferior spelling and oral reading habits, developing primarily from difficulties in pronunciation, was found in one case and was somewhat probable in another.

The first case had an I. Q. of 116, was up to the average of his grade (Grade IV) in speed of silent reading of easy material, but was the poorest in his grade in oral reading and spelling. His perceptual abilities were about average. He was better than the average in proof-reading, and was exactly at the mean in recognition spelling.

In oral reading, the subject read with great rapidity and not badly when the material was easy, but when unfamiliar words were encountered a more or less similar word, or a jumble of sounds, was often rapidly articulated. His reading of a difficult passage was a meaningless series of correct reactions to the easy words with unintelligible pronunciation of the difficult. In spelling, the difficult words were guessed at in a hurried fashion.

The interpretation suggested is that embarrassment was occasioned by the subject's speech difficulties, which were exaggerated by slow responses and hesitation. Rather than slowing down to study the difficult words in oral reading or spelling, the habit of keeping the articulation going while the going was good had been developed to the neglect of systematic or careful analytical work. The result was a habit fixation of ineffective methods of attack.

A careful study of the mispronunciation of words often gives a cue to the misspellings; e.g., such spellings as "vister," "ketch," "factry," "estermate," "proaches," "rangement." Such individual peculiarities and the occasional general tendency to mispronunciation offer possibilities for useful teaching devices, but they were found to be of little diagnostic significance except that serious difficulties in pronunciation or seriously incorrect or slurred pronunciations sometimes show a close and important relation to poor spelling. Samples of such cases will be considered in the final chapter.

4. Alleged Defects of Visual Imagery

It is frequently said that poor spellers cannot adequately "visualize" the words; that the proper training consists in strengthening the "powers of visualization," and, if this procedure fails, defective powers are indicated. The visual image, despite prodigious work on it, is still very much a mystery. No one knows precisely what it is, on what mechanisms it depends, or how to measure it with accuracy. The technique now available is quite inadequate to yield reliable results with children.[2] The introspective method was clearly beyond the capacities of the children tested, and none of the objective methods yielded information which seemed either reliable or significant.

In our procedure the image has been conceived as a symptom of the perceptual reaction. When the word is appropriately perceived, the image is adequate; when the habit of observation is ineffective,

---

[2] See Fernald, M. R., *The Diagnosis of Mental Imagery*, Psychological Review Monographs, Vol. xiv, No. 1, 1912.

the image is incomplete and vague. In the method of learning to spell, which will be described shortly, one essential step is the effort to recall the visual appearance of the word. This procedure is of assistance in building up appropriate methods of perception, since vagueness, incompleteness and distortions of the image may lead to corrective types of observation. No one can tell just how the child is observing a word; he must learn to do this for himself. This effort to recall the appearance of a word is a good device. The image is thus not conceived as an end in itself, but as a kind of reflection of the effectiveness of observation.

The discussion of other possible causes of difficulty in spelling will be taken up in the last chapter.

D. DESCRIPTION OF A METHOD OF TEACHING SPELLING USED IN GRADES III TO VI INCLUSIVE

The form of instruction adopted in Grades III to VI inclusive, at various dates late in November or early in December, will be shown in the following selections taken for the most part, from an eight-page mimeographed pamphlet which was distributed among the teachers.

ADMINISTRATION OF TESTS AND LESSONS

1. *First Step.* Take 20–30 consecutive words from the list for a test. On the record sheet, write the name of a pupil above each column. Down the left hand-side, enter the words in order. For example:

Name	1	2	3	4	5	6	etc.
day	C	C	√	√	C	C	
eat	√	C	C	√	C	√	
sit	C	√	√	√	C	√	
lot	C	√	C	√	C	C	

Read off the words for the test. When the papers are corrected the results should be entered in the table as follows: *C* for correct, √ for incorrect. On later trials or reviews add another check for an error, or a *C* if correct.

2. The words missed by each pupil should form his spelling project for the week. He should write each word on a card and study it as suggested later, until learned. Keep the unlearned words in

an envelope or box marked "words to learn." When mastered, the card should be transferred to an envelope or box marked "words to be reviewed."

3. On Tuesday, Wednesday, etc., each child studies his own group of words. When he has mastered his set, he should take the next 10 or so words from the list, write them on cards and study them as before. The teacher should credit the pupil with a *C* on her list when he has mastered his Monday failures.

4. On Friday, the teacher gives a review test, made up of the words most frequently misspelled on the Monday test. All words then missed must be relearned.

5. On Monday, give a test of 20 or more words next in order on the list and so on.

6. The teacher will find that it is not a difficult task to keep a class record as suggested. It is most useful. She can discover at a glance the status of the class as a whole and the precise attainment and special difficulties of each child. She can easily discover how rapidly to advance, how many new words to assign, what words to include in a review, what pupils to encourage. It is often most wise to post the list for the inspection of the children. The list should be kept since it will be of decided value to the succeeding teacher.

Learning to spell should become an individual project which the pupil undertakes largely on his own initiative. He should set out to make of himself a proficient speller, as one sets out to make himself a football player, a singer, or a builder of houses. No one would be most proficient in any line without first *being taught how to proceed*, and when young he will need encouragement, guidance, and correction. Left entirely to his own inclinations, the child will not always learn the things that are best for him, and he is almost certain not to acquire the best methods of learning. This is true of spelling as it is notoriously true of typewriting, swimming, and many other functions.

1. Carefully pronounce the printed word by syllables or in units convenient for pronunciation. For example: *nev-er, fil-a-ment, cur-tain, cer-tain, nup-tials.* Look at each syllable very carefully during pronunciation.

2. Next, look aside or close your eyes if you like, and as you pronounce the word syllable by syllable, try to think how the word looks. If you cannot remember how each syllable looks, glance at the word. Keep trying until you can "visualize" the word clearly.

3. Now write the word on paper while pronouncing it syllable by syllable. If you fail, try to think how the word looks. If you cannot do that, look at the printed word again. Repeat step 2 before trying again to write it, however. When you have written the word once, compare it with the printed word. If correct, cover it up and write it several times, always looking at it closely and pronouncing the syllables to yourself.

4. If the word was difficult, put it in the group for review and try it again the next day.

SUPPLEMENTARY SUGGESTIONS

1. Careful articulation of the word is of great importance. Investigations show a constant tendency to spell a word as it is pronounced: "git" for "get," "orfice" for "office," "afterwoods" for "afterwards," "farther" for "father," "whent" for "went," etc. Phonic training is sometimes the means of correcting the spelling. The child spells "dorter" "aftah," "perticler," "walkin" because he hears and pronounces it that way. Judge the correctness of hearing by his pronunciation and correct the sound by sounding the word carefully for him.

2. More frequently the trouble lies in improperly observing the word. Misspellings of *assist*, such as "aisst," "asast," "acist," "asist," etc., are due not to phonic or articulatory difficulties, but to inadequate visual perception of the word. This is the

---

[1] The method described is very similar to that devised by Horn, E. and Ashbaugh, E. J. See *Lippincott's Horn-Ashbaugh Speller*. Philadelphia: J. B. Lippincott, 1921. See also Tidyman, W. F., *The Teaching of Spelling*, pp. 145-151, for other methods. Yonkers: World Book Co., 1919.

most common type of difficulty. The method of careful observation plus visualization aims to develop an appropriate method of observing words.

3. Syllabication is desirable. In the sense of careful pronunciation of the word syllables it is very desirable. Emphasis on syllables visually (visual analysis) is also desirable especially in Grades I, II, and III, in connection with reading, since in these years children often fail to see the word elements clearly. The analysis should be made in terms of syllables, not letters, or phonetic elements. The pupil should learn to spell (recall) as they study, i.e., syllable by syllable, not letter by letter, or in any unsystematic way. Reciting aloud by letters is not a helpful procedure. Writing is far superior. Syllabication is superior to letter-by-letter spelling. Many cases of poor spelling are traced to the letter habit. Oral spelling is usually found to be less productive. Finally, real life seldom demands oral spelling.

4. Writing the word is the final purpose. All other means should guide to this end since in life's activities we need to spell so we may write. Writing in the air is less effective than writing on paper and provides no useful practice in writing. Making the handwriting movements with the blunt end of a pen or pencil offers no opportunity for a check on accuracy of spelling. It is useful to detect errors in spelling (or better to teach the child to do so) in regular written composition, history, etc., lessons. The child must learn to spell while attending to the content.

5. The amount of repetitions of the sort suggested will vary greatly from pupil to pupil and from word to word. The pupil must be convinced that to learn the word so he can just write it is not enough. He should repeat it several times thereafter.

6. The pupil should know the meaning of the word he is learning to spell.

7. Spelling rules should be used sparingly, unless the teacher has a great deal of confidence in particular ones. Ordinarily, spelling rules seem to have very little value.

8. No form of word grouping (sound, look, meaning, etc.) has proved to be of value. Any advantage is immediate and fails

to show itself later. Such groupings often lead to inclusion of words which the child does not need to spell.

9. Groupings by similarities of error, specially in review, are sometimes effective, but seldom worth the trouble.

10. Calling attention to special portions of words by underlining colored letters, etc., has not been found generally useful.

11. Diacritical marks should not be used. Diacritical marks merely add to the amount to be learned and are foreign to children's interests. As a rule, they retard rather than accelerate progress in spelling. Not one pupil in a hundred will make use of the diacritical marks after leaving school.

12. For the general progress of the group, an aggressive interest is essential. The plan here outlined aims at securing that, but skillful encouragement by a teacher is equally important. Generally, when the pupil is taught how to learn to spell, and is shown what he should spell and what he cannot spell, he will respond by an enthusiastic endeavor to handle the project, and handle it well, on his own initiative.

13. Learning to spell words used in out-of-school activities should be encouraged. One purpose of teaching a definite method is to provide for initiative in properly learning to spell whenever or wherever the need occurs. It would be an excellent thing to encourage pupils to write out each new word on a card, learn it and bring the cards to school. The teacher should keep a record of words thus learned by each pupil, and reward such initiative, in the lower grades at least, by posting the words independently learned.

The form of training for perception in reading, described in the preceding chapter, and the devices described here, supplement each other. Together they are expected to develop a method of attack and a form of perception which will contribute to effective reading, during which the bonds involved in spelling will be constantly strengthened, as well as during the spelling lesson.

E. IMPROVEMENT IN SPELLING ABILITY

1. GROSS IMPROVEMENT BY GRADES

Tests made up of 50 words from the Ayres-Buckingham Scale were given to all grades in early November.[4] Soon after this, the method of teaching spelling, just described, was placed in the hands of the teachers, and put into effect in Grades III to VI inclusive at various dates late in November or early in December. Since practically no specific instruction in spelling was given in Grades VII and VIII, the results for these grades afford a basis of comparison. The amount of time given to spelling by the lower grades was somewhat less than the average time given to this subject by American schools.

TABLE XXX

SCORES IN SPELLING TESTS IN TERMS OF PERCENTAGE OF CORRECT SPELLING OF EQUIVALENT LISTS SELECTED FROM AYRES-BUCKINGHAM SCALE

Figures in column 4 are improvements expressed in terms of average improvements achieved by American schools in general (Ayres norms). Grades III–VI used the special method

GRADE	1 SCORE NOVEMBER 1	2 SCORE JANUARY 15	3 SCORE MAY 15	4 IMPROVEMENT IN YEARS
III	21	40	55	1.7
IV	29	52	69	1.8
V	42	63	82	2.2
VI	40	57	70	2.0

Grades VII and VIII had little specific instruction in spelling

| VII | 61 | 63 | 66 | 0.4 |
| VIII | 59 | 62 | 64 | 0.4 |

The improvement in spelling which resulted primarily from the teaching during three-fourths or less of the school year, are given in Table XXX, in terms of the average yearly improvements in schools in general, as determined by Ayres.[5] In most grades, the improve-

[4] The list comprised 5 words from 10 columns, beginning with the 92 per cent and ending with the 34 per cent column, giving an average difficulty equal to the 66 per cent list for each grade.

[5] Ayres, L. P., *A Measuring Scale for Ability in Spelling*. New York: Russell Sage Foundation. 1915.

ment was more than twice that made by average schools in the same time. This improvement cannot be attributed to any single cause; the method of teaching reading as well as spelling, the motivation, the demand for improvement, etc., probably each made some contribution; but the fact remains that very great absolute improvements were achieved. Some pupils, in particular, were brought from a state of apparent "backwardness" or "inability" into reasonably good spelling ability. Given a method of attack and stimulated to make a start, some of the pupils, earlier discouraged or chagrined by failure, developed new interest with increased achievement.

2. Correlations of Initial Ability with Final Ability and Amount of Improvement

Table XXXI gives the correlations between ability in November and in May, and the correlation of ability at the start with the gross

TABLE XXXI

Correlation between (1) Spelling Ability in November and (2) Spelling Ability in May

Grade	1 November with May	2 November with Improvement
III	.83	—.70
IV	.80	—.69
V	.85	—.75
VI	.62	—.55
MEAN	.78	—.67
VII	.92	—.32
VIII	.89	—.21
MEAN	.91	—.27

amount of improvement during the year. Since spelling was not taught to any great extent in Grades VII and VIII as a whole, these results are grouped separately.

Although the teachers doubtless gave more attention to poor spellers than to good spellers in their classes, the relative positions of pupils at the end of the year are about the same as they were at the beginning. The mean correlation for Grades VII and VIII

(0.91) is somewhat higher than the mean for Grades III to VI, which is 0.78.

Column (2), Table XXXI, shows, however, a high negative correlation between ability in November and the amount of improvement during the year. A number of factors conspire to bring this about. Some of the pronounced backwardness was due largely to sheer lack of methods of learning to spell. When they were taught how to learn to spell and when they found they were really learning, their interest as well as their ability improved, with the result that they made enormous progress during the year. For example, in terms of percentage of words spelled of lists of equal difficulty, in November and in May, certain Grade III pupils changed from 0 to 42, 3 to 67, 0 to 40, 2 to 45, etc. They were not, however, able to overtake their originally more able classmates. The negative correlations are considerably higher in the lower grades than in Grades VII and VIII, where spelling was emphasized less. Other factors are involved in these correlations, one important one being the fact that the improvement of the more able pupils in the several grades was not adequately measured. It was possible to increase 40 per cent if the initial score was low, but not if it was high. The range of scores in the May test was consequently much less than in November, but the range of real ability may have been as great or greater.

3. INABILITY TO LEARN TO SPELL OR "SPECIAL DISABILITY" IN SPELLING

Study of the records of individuals shows that none of the poor spellers failed to improve and that with the exception of three cases, all final scores were above 40. The norm for each grade, according to Ayres' data, is 66. On general principles we would expect even with effective methods of learning that individuals will differ widely in native aptitude for forming the particular associations involved in the mastery of spelling. While most of our pupils improved greatly, some of them will probably never become highly proficient. The term "disability" has been applied to certain cases which possess approximately zero ability to acquire these particular bonds and some evidence indicates that such cases do exist.[6]

We have found but one case so far which seems to represent

[6] See Hollingworth, L. S., *The Psychology of Special Disability in Spelling.*

a native incapacity—the fag end of the curve of distribution—for forming the connections necessary to spell words. This case was a Grade III pupil, a fair reader but very poor speller, whose score was zero on the November test, 6 in January, and 16 in May. He had profited but little from intensive training in phonics given by his teacher. He could spell no word containing more than three letters. He was equally poor in written and oral spelling. The disability seemed to bear no relation to hearing, vision, or general intelligence, all of which were normal. His perceptual abilities with words— recognition spelling, proof-reading, etc.—were in the vicinity of the 30 percentile of his grade. The outstanding fact was that he could not learn or if he learned he could not retain the spelling of words with anything like average readiness. Although this subject will doubtless never learn to spell with ease, the writer is not yet convinced that no remedy can be found which will considerably increase his ability to learn. Unfortunately, the subject moved before we were able to undertake further studies that were planned, so that we cannot confidently render the diagnosis of native "disability."

Two other cases, while showing steady improvement, learn with much less than average dispatch and retain poorly. These will be the subjects of further study.

In the next chapter, a more extensive discussion of the causes of backwardness and difficulty in spelling (and reading) will be undertaken.

F. SUMMARY

A. The Influence of the Type of Word Perception.

    1. Correlations show that word-perception is an important factor in the determination of success in spelling.

    2. The most common cause of misspelling is to be found in inadequacy of acquaintance with the visual form of the word.

    3. Inability to make an analytical attack upon unfamiliar words is typical of the poor speller.

B. Comparison of Ability to Recognize Words with Ability to Recall (spell) Words.

    1. The two functions show a correlation of 0.6.

    2. Recognition exceeds recall in 96 cases out of 100.

3. The differences between Recognition and Recall vary similarly for good and poor spellers.

4. The spelling of words must first be acquired by specific practice.

5. When once acquired, the spelling of words is relearned to some extent by those subjects who perceive words in a certain clear and effective way, during the course of ordinary reading.

C. The Relation of Spelling to the Form of Motor Reaction.

1. One may learn to spell by articulation, writing, "visual imagery," typewriting, or in other ways. Man's native capacity to learn favors no form of motor reaction.

2. In ordinary testing, the word will be spelled most successfully by the motor reaction involved in learning. Among our subjects, written spelling exceeds oral spelling, specially in the upper grades, for this reason.

3. Although the correlation of writing ability with spelling ability is but +0.12, extreme deficiency of the former handicaps the subject in learning to spell. Often poor writing and spelling have common causes. (See Chapter VIII.)

4. Speech defects may contribute to inadequacy of spelling as well as reading.

5. Defects of visual imagery cannot be accurately diagnosed and are believed to be a reflection of inadequate perception rather than primary in character.

D. Description of a Method of Learning to Spell.

1. The method is designed to function conjointly with the training in word perception described under reading.

2. It comprises direct practice in pronunciation and visual study by syllables or more inclusive units, with a device for checking accuracy by "visualizing" and by writing. It purposes to secure (1) appropriate habits of visual perception of words, (2) correct pronunciation, (3) ability for independent analytical attack, and (4) final mastery through writing.

    3. Spelling rules, word groupings, diacritical marks, etc., are used very sparingly.

E. Improvement in Spelling.

    1. The various classes using the above method improved more than twice as much as similar classes in the average school.

    2. While many of the initially poor spellers made relatively large gross gains, the correlation between initial and final abilities was very high.

CHAPTER VIII

THE CAUSES OF BACKWARDNESS IN READING AND SPELLING

In the previous sections, interest has centered mainly in discovery of the precise functions in which the good readers and spellers differ from the poor. In this chapter will be summarized the outstanding deficiencies of the backward cases, together with considerations of the more ultimate causal factors.

Reading or spelling a word is a tremendously complicated function, involving a large number of bodily mechanisms and subject to a wide variety of influences which are interrelated so complexly that the search for the causes of backwardness offers difficulties that are many and momentous. At this stage of diagnosis, errors are doubtless frequent, and it is not likely, furthermore, that all possible causes of difficulty in these functions will be disclosed by the particular group studied.

The causal factors which seemed probable or possible will be reviewed under the following heads and in the order indicated.

A. Unfavorable Training and Environmental Influences.
B. Unfavorable Behavior of a General Character.
C. Defects of the Sensory Mechanisms.
D. Defects of the Motor Mechanisms.
E. Defects of the Connecting Mechanisms.

A. UNFAVORABLE TRAINING AND ENVIRONMENTAL INFLUENCES

1. *Neglect of training in visual perception of words.* Learning wholly by the "natural" method or "word" method or otherwise without training in visual perception or analysis results frequently in inappropriate methods of observing words. This occurred among pupils who had superior intelligence and no organic or physical defects which could be discovered; who were anxious to learn and had, some of them, devoted unusual amounts of time to the effort. The types of difficulties found among such cases were various. For example:

a. Mis-recognition and mispronunciation due to habits of perceiving words rather vaguely as wholes, or by perceiving clearly only certain parts.

b. Inability for or ineffective methods of attacking unfamiliar words.

c. Habits of neglecting unfamiliar words accompanied by a search through the material in an effort to comprehend on the basis of such words as were familiar.

d. Mispronunciation of familiar words because of (c).

e. Various types of inappropriate eye-movements as a result of (a), (b) and (c).

f. Narrow eye-voice span due to (a), (b) and (c).

g. Failure to comprehend because attention was absorbed in effort to recognize or pronounce.

2. *Inappropriate forms of phonic, phonetic or other types of analytical training* result frequently in unfavorable types of perception and in other ineffective habits. For example:

a. Super-sufficient reaction to details of words, resulting in slow, laborious reading, in a variety of errors, in inability to grasp sufficiently large units of words, and in inability to attack long words effectively.

b. Placement of emphasis on wrong characteristics of words, or dividing words in ways ineffective for ready recognition.

c. Progressing by too small units which may lead to inappropriate habits of eye movements.

d. Habits of too explicit articulation which may lead to an inhibition of the development of speed in silent reading.

e. Habits of reacting primarily by efforts to pronounce accurately which may lead to inadequacy of comprehension.

f. Habits of not looking ahead in reading, i. e., too narrow eye-voice span.

3. *Changes from one form of phonic, phonetic or visual training to another* may have resulted in inhibitions or confusions which prevented the formation of effective perceptual habits, although it is

usually impossible to tell whether the *change* of training or the effects of some inappropriate form of training is causal.

4. *The effects of early training in foreign languages.*   That early training in a foreign language is occasionally the cause of backwardness in reading and spelling has been suggested by several workers.[1] The backwardness of one of our cases whose earlier years were spent in a country where Spanish is spoken, may have been so caused, but it was impossible to develop this hypothesis with any certainty. No physical defects could be found to account for her perceptual difficulties, but whether sheer lack of training, improper training, or the influence of the foreign language or some other factor was causal, we were unable to discover. Since few subjects studied came from homes in which foreign languages were customarily spoken, but meager data on this factor were secured.

5. *Unfavorable home training.*   In several cases, home conditions of an unfavorable sort may have contributed to backwardness in reading and spelling. One case affords an instructive example. This pupil seldom read for herself at home, the parent or governess reading aloud the newspapers, fiction, and even the school lessons. The parental defense for this practice was that the child had always found reading difficult. What the real cause of the difficulty was, we were unable to discover since other defects and deficiencies were found, but lack of practice had apparently not improved her interest or ability.

6. *Irregular attendance, illness, change of schools, home instruction of unfavorable sorts occurring at critical periods* in the process of learning, may contribute considerably to real difficulty in reading. For example: one pupil was reported as making normal progress in Grade II, but was removed from school for four months at about the time analytical training was begun. On returning to school, the child's failure to read the material then used in oral reading occasioned embarrassment leading to habits of rapid, conjectural, slurring procedure that became fixed, inhibiting his progress. In other cases, it appeared that loss of schooling or a change of schools had been a predecessor of difficulty, although, of course, one could not say with certainty that it had been the cause.

---

[1] Hollingworth, L. S., *op. cit.*, and Gray, W. S., "Diagnostic and Remedial Steps in Reading." *Journal of Educational Research*, June, 1921.

B. BACKWARDNESS DUE TO UNFAVORABLE BEHAVIOR
OF A GENERAL CHARACTER

1. *Disinclination, inertia, etc.* Under this caption a large number
of factors, such as sheer laziness, distaste for school or for mental
work, emotional disturbance, temporary or chronic, outside interests, home spoiling, illness, removals, malnutrition, etc., might be
considered. Without doubt some of the backwardness found was
due to lack of interest and effort, however occasioned. Disinclination sometimes was caused by inability, which in turn was due to
ineffective methods or native inaptitude. The function was disliked
because it was difficult, because little progress attended application,
and because of the chagrin of constant failure. When the pupil had
acquired effective methods of study and observed that he really
could learn, a new and happy interest was the common result. Some
of the pupils, for example, began to read books, a thing that had
never previously been done because reading was difficult work.
Several cases, however, especially in spelling, failed to develop any
considerable interest or initiative. To discover the ultimate cause of
such disinclination would require a more intimate acquaintance
with the life history and heredity of these cases than we were able
to secure.

2. *Emotional or nervous instability.* That the unstable or neurotic child is frequently retarded in school work, even when general
intelligence is high, has been noted. In a study of unstable children,
Burt, for example, reports: "Arithmetic is invariably their worst
subject. . . . Spelling is commonly weak—reading is fluent and
expressive, but full of guess work and inaccuracy—they have no
patience for the slow and systematic procedure of phonic analysis—
writing is irregular and untidy."[1] Such backwardness is explained ᴠ
to be the result of defective apperception, attention, etc., which invariably accompany the neurotic constitution. "Ordinary school
work calls for precisely those qualities of character and intellect in
which they are conspicuously lacking." "They are not necessarily
lazy, though frequently accused of laziness." . . . "where interest
is caught they work with feverish zeal in fits and starts."

Two cases have come to our attention in which general excita-
bility, nervousness and other symptoms suggestive of instability

---

[1] Cyril Burt, "The Unstable Child," *Child Study* (London), Oct. 1917, p. 71.

have been associated with backwardness in spelling and arithmetic particularly. These children were unable or unwilling to apply themselves to rote learning for more than very short periods.[3] They were hasty and careless in learning and in their responses during test. Methods of studying were neither effective nor consistent, but both subjects were able to learn to spell with fair facility during short periods of trial. They tired of the work very readily. Both were rapid, but inaccurate in reading, mispronunciation of familiar words being frequent. Depth of comprehension indicated by the Thorndike-McCall test was as great as would be expected for children of their general mental ability. Their achievement in content subjects, history, geography, etc., was likewise satisfactory.

The writings of specialists in the field of instability among children give but few suggestions concerning the educational treatment of such cases, and there is not complete agreement among those given. All would doubtless agree upon (1) special hygiene measures and the avoidance of exciting causes of emotional or nervous disturbances, (2) the development of varieties of devices to make the school tasks interesting, (3) frequent change of tasks, and (4) the development of optimum methods of learning.[4]

C. DEFECTS OF SENSORY MECHANISMS

1. *Defects of vision.* Vision was tested at least roughly by the group test V 1, V 2, V 5, V 6, V 7 and V 8 earlier described. When a pupil did poorly in all of these tests, motor defects having been eliminated, he was referred to an oculist for further examination. Four cases have been encountered in which visual defects were probably primarily responsible for backwardness in reading and spelling. It is quite possible that defective vision, unnoticed at the time of initial efforts to read, was responsible in other cases for the development of inappropriate habits which persisted after correction. It is obviously impossible in such cases to determine the facts with certainty. In any case of backwardness in reading or spelling a thorough examination of the eyes should be made.

2. *Defects of hearing.* Hearing was tested only when some reason for an examination was suggested in the course of the work. For

---

[3] See also Hollingworth, L. S., *op. cit.*, pp. 68 ff.

[4] See Burt, Cyril, *op. cit.*, or Terman, L. M., *The Hygiene of the School Child*, Chap. XXVIII. Boston: Houghton Mifflin, 1914.

acuity, the simple watch test was used.[5] Several cases were tested for pitch discrimination by use of tuning forks [6] and by some of the Seashore graphophone tests.[7] Tests of ability to spell certain simple phonic units—nub, sug, rip, etc.—were generally used.

We have found but one case in which auditory difficulty appeared to bear a relation to difficulty in reading. This subject was unable to discriminate pitches differing by less than about 38 vibrations per seconds (30 vs. is about a half tone) and did very poorly in all tests of auditory discrimination. His articulation was faulty, although this was said to be due partly to motor as well as auditory difficulties. He had difficulty in phonics at school and was, as a matter of fact, rather poor in our tests of simple phonic spelling. He was said to be poor also in "auditory memory," but we did not find this to be true except in so far as difficulties in hearing and articulation reduced his score, although in spelling he made many such errors as "have" for "half," "afaid" for "afraid." Two types of remedial work were suggested: (1) careful training in pronunciation, and (2) training in word-perception. He improved steadily but not brilliantly.

There is still uncertainty with regard to the causal factors involved in this case. Whether the auditory deficiency or the articulatory deficiency are directly responsible, or whether they were indirectly responsible through setting up inappropriate habits; whether central factors were involved or whether this was simply another case of inappropriate training (auditory defects being largely incidental) only further investigation will disclose.

There is prevalent among workers in this field an unfortunate tendency to accept unhesitatingly as causes of linguistic and other difficulties, almost any deficiency that is found. "Defects of auditory powers" and "auditory memory" are frequently given. For example, in the two cases given in a recent book by Cyril Burt,[8] one is diagnosed as due to "feeble auditory powers" and "defects in auditory perception and memory"; the other to similar defects of "visual powers." In neither case is the evidence satisfactory

[5] See Whipple, G. M., *Manual of Physical and Mental Tests*, Part 1, pp. 200–213.
[6] Whipple, *op. cit.*, pp. 213–223.
[7] Seashore, C. E., *The Psychology of Musical Talent*.
[8] Burt, Cyril, *Mental and Scholastic Tests*, pp. 286 ff. London: P. S. King and Son, 1921.

and, on closer examination, other unsuspected defects may be found.[9]

D. DEFECTS OF MOTOR MECHANISMS

1. *Defects in general motor coordination and control.* Aside from the writing tests, no systematic examinations of general motor control were made. The maze tracing test and the instruments for estimating steadiness and precision of motor control would have been desirable supplements. In one case of backwardness in spelling with mild backwardness in reading, a general clumsiness and inco-ordination of motor control was found. In this case the exceptional superiority of oral over written spelling was found to be due to difficulty in writing, together with slow and laborious oral reading, occasioned in part, probably, by difficulty in articulation. In two other cases, written spelling was inferior to oral because difficulty in writing had led to lack of practice in the former. A fourth case of decided backwardness in reading and spelling showed conspicuous inferiority in motor control, which displayed itself in poor writing, catchy, halting articulation with stammer, and general clumsiness of hand. This case was observed but once for less than an hour so that little weight can be given to an estimate of the effect of these difficulties.

2. *Defective writing ability* when not associated with general motor incoordination, whether due to native inaptitude or failure to hit upon effective methods, seems to be in certain cases associated with backwardness in spelling, although the correlation of spelling with writing is but $+0.18$. Often, the association of poor spelling and writing is due to some other common cause, such as disinclination, habitual carelessness, etc. Many poor spellers are good writers and many poor writers are good spellers, but in diagnosis the writing should be carefully studied for the infrequent cases where a real causal relation exists.

3. *Defective articulation* was, according to our appraisal, definitely associated with one case of inferior reading and spelling. The causal connection was indirect, since it appeared that habits of hurrying, for the purpose of avoiding the embarrassment attending a slight stammer which occurred when the subject encountered difficulty,

[9] See Fildes, L. G., "A Psychological Inquiry into the Nature of the Condition Known as Congenital Word-Blindness," *Brain*, Nov. 1921.

had led to a variety of inappropriate habits which inhibited the development of effective methods of attack. A similar solution was suggested, although uncertain in a second case.

4. *Defective eye-muscle control.* Two cases of defective visual perception grew out of defective coordination of the eye-muscles which was not discovered until strabismus developed. One of these subjects was reported by an oculist to have "defective convergence and word-blindness." Following correction and remedial treatment of the oculo-motor defect, this subject rapidly learned to read and spell as a result of training in word perception and analysis. The former subject improved much more slowly, due in part, probably, to a continued difficulty in control of eye movements, and, in part, to the persistence of certain unfavorable reading habits.

5. *Inappropriare eye-movements,* in cases showing no organic defect, usually accompany all types of difficulty in reading. It appeared, in the cases here studied, that the inappropriate eye habits were secondary; a necessary result of difficulty in reading, however caused. We were unable to alleviate the difficulty in any case tried, by means of training directed to eye-movements alone. On the other hand, the facility with which eye-movements readjusted themselves as the result of improvement in reading achieved by other forms of training was very great.

6. *Inappropriate eye-voice span.* Like inappropriate eye-movements, a limited eye-voice span (inability to look ahead of the words being silently or audibly articulated) seems to be a symptom or result of other difficulties rather than the cause of them.

E. DEFECTS OR DEFICIENCIES OF THE CONNECTING MECHANISMS

1. *General mental ability.* Just what level of mental ability is necessary to reading and spelling is not very accurately known. Since none of our subjects was of low I. Q., no data on this matter were secured. Even among the groups whose I. Q.'s averaged about 117, the correlation of reading ability with general mental ability measured by the Stanford M. A. ranged from 0.30 to 0.71, and the correlation between reading and the scores on a composite of verbal group test ranged from 0.60 to 0.80. Correlations between spelling and Stanford M. A. averaged 0.31; between spelling and verbal group tests, 0.42.

Among unselected children, backwardness in reading and spelling will probably be more frequently associated with low general mental ability than with any other single cause. An I. Q. of 70 is probably the minimum essential to comprehensive reading.

2. *Congenital defects of special cortical areas.* In the earlier literature on inability to learn to read or spell, the source of the trouble is frequently ascribed to "some damage to the visual word center in early childhood," or to "congenital localized neural lesions" or more specifically "congenital word-blindness," "congenital alexia," and "Amnesia Visualis Verbalis," etc.

Bronner, as a result of studies of backwardness in reading, states: "At the present stage of our knowledge there is no establishing by symptoms the fact of congenital localized neural lesions or defects analogous to acquired lesions."[10] With regard to spelling, L. S. Hollingworth writes: "The thesis suggested by psychological examination of these extreme cases, and by the total work done with poor spellers in our experimental class is that ability to spell is a complex trait, which distributes itself over a normal distribution curve; and that the rare extreme cases described as "congenital word blindness," etc., form the very fag end of this normal distribution."[11] Freeman writes: "We seem justified in raising a serious question whether there is such a thing as specific congenital word-blindness or alexia."[12]

There can be no doubt that ophthalmologists and oculists are generally wrong in their diagnoses of congenital word-blindness. Three cases coming to our attention had been so diagnosed, but in all of these appropriate instruction enabled them to learn, one of them with very great rapidity.

A recent and intensive survey of the localizations of functions of the central nervous system is extremely cautious on this problem and offers no cases considered as authentic evidence.[13] It would appear that while such congenital localized defects are possibilities they are extremely rare in occurrence.

While most psychologists engaged in this field of diagnosis have, as indicated above, shown considerable eagerness to avoid the

[10] Bronner, *The Psychology of Special Abilities and Disabilities*, p. 88.
[11] Hollingworth, L. S., *Psychology of Special Disability in Spelling*, p. 95.
[12] Freeman, F. N., "Clinical Study as a Method in Experimental Education," *Journal of Applied Psychology*, March, 1920, p. 136.
[13] Tilney, F. and Riley, H. A., *The Form and Functions of the Central Nervous System*, New York, 1921.

implications of the concepts involved in "congenitally localized defects," some of their own diagnoses are no less vague and indeed, in some cases, they have become even more involved in questionable neurological hypotheses.

3. *Defects of "visual memory," "auditory memory," "inability to associate auditory and visual symbols,"* and the like, are often given in diagnosis by some of those workers who have been most vigorous in throwing out of court such concepts as "congenital word-blindness." [14] To the writer, the former concepts are more mysterious than the latter.

Just what can be the basis of such general defects as these? Seldom is an answer attempted. Since they are not the result of low general intelligence (at least, not in these instances) or to visual or auditory defects, they must be due to some sort of defect or deficiency of the central nervous system. The defect, it would appear, must be due to lesion, "isolation," "primary diability," "lowered vitality," [15] or to some other deficiency or defect similar to those considered to be the bases of "alexia." It is really more difficult to conceive of "defects of auditory memory" and the like than defects of word centers for the reason that the former are tremendously more complex and less well localized.

Such concepts, moreover, are quite out of accord with present-day principles of psychology. Memory is not conceived as a unitary faculty or process. On the contrary opinion favors specialization of memories into as many varieties as there are varieties of data.

Study of the evidence of these writers [16] shows, whenever sufficiently comprehensive examinations were made, that as a matter of fact no deficiency of memory in general or of "visual" or "auditory" memory appeared, but rather inadequacy of dealing with certain kinds of data. In some cases, the defect should not have been attributed to *memory* at all.

4. *Defects or deficiencies of general visual perception or discrim-*

[14] For example, see Bronner, *op. cit.*, Chap. VI, and Burt, *Mental and Scholastic Tests*, pp. 286 ff.

[15] See Head, H., "Aphasia and Kindred Disorders of Speech," *Brain*, 1920, pp. 87–165; Head, H., "Disorders of Symbolic Thinking and Expression," *British Journal of Psychology (Genl.)*, Jan., 1921; Mourgue, R., "Disorders of Symbolic Thinking due to Local Lesions of the Brain," *British Journal of Psychology (Medical)*, Jan., 1921; and Fildes. L. G., "A Psychological Inquiry into the Nature of the Condition Known as Congenital Word-blindness," *Brain*, Nov., 1921.

[16] For example see Bronner, *op. cit.*, Chap. VI.

ination,—"visualization." Bronner and others sometimes speak of the association of poor reading and spelling with "defects of visual powers," "powers of visualization," "defective visual perception" or "discrimination," "defects of the auditory visual region." [17] It is not always clear just what is meant by some of these terms, but that *general powers* of visual or auditory perception or "visualization" are often meant is suggested by the context or by the adoption of *general* training of perception or visualization as remedial treatment.

The neurological bases are seldom referred to in these cases, except in a general way such as "primary disability of the auditory or visual regions." Such conceptions are obviously in the same class with "congenital word-blindness" and "general defects of "visual memory."

Among our subjects, not a single case was found in which any general perceptual difficulty (except those due to sensory defects) appeared nor was there any association of poor reading and spelling with generally inferior perceptual abilities. The good readers and spellers were no better than the poor in perceptual abilities involving pictures, geometrical figures, digits and letters as materials. When a subject did poorly in all tests of perception, the cause was found to be defective vision, eye-muscle control, general motor incoordination, nervous instability, etc.

Instead of a general perceptual ability, our evidence indicates specialized abilities to perceive certain classes of items. Substantially positive correlations were found among various forms of perceptual reactions to similar materials, e.g., words, digits, etc., whereas correlations were low when the materials were different even if the form of the functions was the same.

5. *Defects of "visual imagery."* Defects in "visual imagery" to which defective spelling is sometimes attributed are even greater mysteries. No one knows precisely what imagery is, on what mechanisms it depends, or how to examine it accurately in children. The imagery is probably best considered as a symptom of perceptual reactions. When the habits of observation of words are ineffective, the imagery is incomplete, vague and perhaps distorted. In teaching children to learn to spell, one essential step consists in the effort to recall the appearance of the word just observed. This

[17] See also Fildes. *op. cit.*

procedure is of assistance in building up appropriate methods of perception, since vagueness, incompleteness and distortions of the "image" may lead to corrective types of observation. The image is not, however, conceived to be an end in itself but a reflection of the effectiveness of observation. We did not consider that the difficulties were due, therefore, in any case, to specific defects of "power of visual imagery."

6. *The concept of "special disability."* The term "disability" has been variously and loosely used until recently it has acquired a technical significance. As used by Hollingworth it implies a native inability to acquire some or all of the reactions involved in a particular function, e.g., spelling. She contends that "we find a few children of normal intellectual capacity whose spelling ability approaches zero" and that "a few of the very extreme cases of disability will be unable to learn to spell, even with the maximum of effort." [18]

What is the physical basis of such disability? The author states that: "The question is analogous to the question in the case of 'idiocy.' They [idiots] form the lower end of the continuous curve of distribution for human intelligence; they result just as mediocre and superior result from the operation of unknown laws of heredity and variation; and they are no more to be regarded as 'pathological' than are the exceptionally superior individuals, who are as far above mediocrity as they are below it." [19]

It would appear from this analogy with idiocy as well as from Hollingworth's general discussion that "special disability" is not the result of a number or complex of definable bodily defects or deficiencies such as those of the sensory mechanisms, the motor mechanisms (eye muscles, speech muscles, finger muscles, etc.) or more general inadequacies such as instability, nervousness, distaste for drill, or such matters as the unfavorable results of inappropriate training. For example, she states that: "By far the greater proportion of the total sum of bad spelling is due to causes other than special disability—such as intellectual weakness, lack of interest—sensory defects, bad handwriting," etc.[20] It is obvious that "special disability" is to be contrasted with and distinguished from such sources of backwardness. It is an inability "to form the bonds in-

[18] *Op. cit.*, pp. 96 f.
[19] *Op. cit.*, p. 96.
[20] *Op. cit.*, p. 74.

volved in learning to spell words." We take it that the basis of such incapacity is to be found in the functions of the central nervous system.

If special disability is "analogous to the case of idiocy," it will be proper to carry this analogy through. Idiocy, at least the primary type ("primary amentia") is commonly ascribed to defects or deficiencies of the nervous substance. Tredgold, for example, summarizes the conditions as follows:

"As compared with the nerve cells of the healthy brain, those of the ament are characterized by the following conditions: (1) numerical deficiency; (2) irregular arrangement; (3) imperfect development of individual cells; and on the whole it may be stated that the amount of change discoverable by the microscope is directly proportionate to the degree of mental deficiency present at birth." [21]

Such descriptions of general deficiencies are entirely intelligible, but to conceive of the situation underlying special disability in spelling or other functions is less easy. Indeed, it is much easier to appreciate the possibility of congenital defect or deficiency of a "word center," "writing center" and the like. There is at least some evidence for the existence of such localizations. It is difficult to picture the neurological condition which might underlie the "inability to form the particular connections involved in spelling" when the subject can read and perform other verbal functions without difficulty.

The writer is therefore not inclined to favor the hypothesis of special disability as framed by Hollingworth. Recent research in localizations of functions by methods of extirpation adds to our skepticism of this hypothesis as well as the concept of "word blindness," "alexia," etc., alleged to be based on congenital defects of particular areas.

The facts of restitution of functions of the central nervous system have long been known [22] even if imperfectly understood. More recently, evidence of substitution and vicarious functioning has become more convincing. For example, Lashley has shown that the destruction of the visual-motor areas of the cortex, or of the striate nucleus of rats does not inhibit the relearning of certain

---

[21] Tredgold, A. F., *Mental Deficiency*, p. 77. New York: William Wood & Co., 1920.
[22] For a comprehensive account, see Ladd, G. T. and Woodworth, R. S., *Elements of Physiological Psychology*, Chap. x. New York: Scribners, 1911.

visual-motor functions.[23] Similarly the destruction of the whole visual-motor area, together with caudate nucleus, does not seriously affect relearning. These experiments "led to the tentative conclusion that the striate nucleus and stimulable cortex have interchangeable functions." [24] Franz, reviewing recent investigations of cerebral localization of functions in man concludes that "although there is a general dependence of mental states upon the state of the brain there is not the defined dependence of a special mental state upon the integrity of certain special cerebral parts." [25]

Evidence of the remarkable capacity for restitution or substitution for disabled brain functions, makes the concept of specialized congenital defects, especially the type required by the hypothesis of "special disability in spelling" or other specialized functions, a very improbable generalization. The analogy of these disabilities with such general conditions, failure of development, etc., as appear to underlie idiocy [26] is fundamentally insecure.

Our attitude should not be interpreted as opposed to the notion of individual differences in native ability for spelling. These differences, according to most substantial evidence, are real and as shown by the data in preceding chapters, they are not removed by special instruction and earnest endeavor. Without a doubt some people always will find certain types of learning difficult, and inherited deficiencies in many cases will be causal.

Our objections have reference to the notion that inability to learn to spell in the case of individuals of normal general intelligence are due *solely* to defects or deficiencies of particular elements of the central nervous system. Such extreme cases, we believe, are to be explained on the basis of a combination of particular unfavorable traits, some of which are quite likely to be overlooked under the limitations of present diagnostic technique.

The enormous complexity of the process of learning to read or spell can scarcely be appreciated in our present state of knowledge.

[23] Lashley, K. S., "Studies of Cerebral Functions in Learning." *Psychobiology*, 1920, 2, 55–135.

[24] Lashley, K. S., "Studies of Cerebral Functions in Learning, No. III. The Motor Areas." *Brain*, Nov. 1921, p. 257.

[25] Franz, S. I., "Cerebral-mental Relations," *Psychological Review*, March, 1921.

[26] For example, it is known that insufficiency of glandular activity may result in the failure of the brain cells to develop. Such deficiency of brain growth is so *general* that to conceive of highly specific effects by similar causes is, according to present knowledge, quite unjustified.

In this, and preceding chapters, some of these factors have been suggested. We should expect from the laws of chance, enormously varying permutations and combinations of these particular abilities. When the infrequent combination of many favorable traits is found, we have an aptitude for spelling; when a similarly complex combination of unfavorable factors is found, we have a "disability" for spelling.

What these unfavorable traits are, is suggested in this chapter, viz., more or less serious deficiencies of vision, hearing, eye-muscle control, lack of training, inappropriate training, varieties of inappropriate habits, home training, poor writing, motor incoordination, specialization of neural organization and perfection, emotionality, nervous instability, inertia, poor health, etc., etc. Some of these deficiencies singly may make learning very difficult, or, indeed, quite inhibit it. A combination of many of them produces the "very fag end of the curve of distribution," whose ability to learn is nearly zero.

While the seriousness of the extreme cases is not overlooked, the explanation here offered implies a quite different attitude with regard to diagnostic and, particularly, remedial treatment.

Concerning the question of fact as to whether there exist cases of normal intelligence who cannot learn to read or spell under proper treatment and instruction, unequivocable data are lacking. Hollingworth's contention that "a few of the very extreme cases of disability will be unable to learn to spell, even with the maximum of effort," was based on the fact that certain children profited but little from twenty weeks of intensive instruction, and on a case of zero ability in reading and spelling in a boy who had received eight years of instruction and private tutoring. It is, of course, possible that these cases were not correctly diagnosed or that the exact remedial treatment needed was not discovered. Freeman believes that "it is doubtful whether there are any children of normal intelligence and vision who are unable to learn to read."[27]

Only extensive investigation will provide a solution. In the present study no cases were found that did not learn to read, although this statement must not be taken to mean that they learned to read as readily as others. Almost certainly, no amount of special training will enable most of our poor readers to equal the achieve-

[27] *Op. cit.,* p. 136.

The Psychology of Reading and Spelling

TABLE XXXII

SUMMARY OF DEFECTS AND DEFICIENCIES FOUND AMONG THE THIRTY
POOREST READERS AND SPELLERS

	READING		SPELLING	
	RATHER MARKED	LESS MARKED	RATHER MARKED	LESS MARKED
A. DEFECTS OR DEFICIENCIES OF TRAINING				
1. Lack of training (chiefly in methods of perceiving words)	10	3	10	3
2. Inappropriate phonic, phonetic, etc., training	7	2	7	2
3. Change of training	6	2	6	2
4. Loss of training at critical periods . . .	4	..	4	..
5. Early training in foreign language . .	1	1	1	1
6. Unfavorable home training (home spoiling, etc.)	3	2	3	2
B. UNFAVORABLE BEHAVIOR; GENERAL				
1. Disinclination, inertia, not otherwise accounted for	2	3	2	3
2. Emotional or nervous instability . . .	2	2	2	2
C. DEFECTS OF SENSORY MECHANISMS (Excluding muscular defects)				
1. Visual	4	3	4	3
2. Auditory	1	2	1	4
D. DEFECTS OF MOTOR MECHANISMS				
1. General motor incoordination, etc. . . .	3	2	3	2
2. Defective writing	1	3	3	2
3. Defective articulation	2	1	2	1
4. Defective eye-muscle control	2	1	2	1
5. Inappropriate eye-movements in reading	15 probably	obably more or	all, but probably not ca	usal
6. Inappropriate eye-voice span	17 probably	obably more, n	ot causal	
E. DEFECTS OR DEFICIENCIES OF CONNECTING MECHANISMS				
1. Inadequate intelligence	None a	mong o	ur subje	cts
2. Congenital word-blindness, alexia, etc.	None a	mong o	ur subje	cts
3. Defects of "visual memory," "auditory memory," etc.	Probab	ly none		
4. Defects of "general visual perception"	None			
5. Defects of "visual imagery"	Probab	ly none		
6. "Special Disability"*	Probab	ly none	—possi	bly one in spelling

* "Special disability" here used in the sense adopted by L. S. Hollingworth, i. e., a specialized deficiency of central nervous system.

ments of the upper quartile. One of our cases made very slow progress in spelling, but because of his departure before the investigation was completed, we are not willing to concede that no method of training would have remedied the difficulty, at least to some extent.

The total number of unselected children from which our special cases were drawn is not known with certainty, but probably, through contacts with the Scarborough School, Horace Mann School and others represented by teacher-students in the writer's classes at Teachers College, as many disabilities as would be found among a thousand school children of average or superior intelligence have been observed. If cases of absolute inability to learn exist, they are, as one would expect, very infrequent among children of normal intelligence.

F. SUMMARY CONCERNING CAUSES OF DIFFICULTY IN READING AND SPELLING

Just where the line should be drawn to mark off cases of "serious difficulty" in these subjects is entirely an arbitrary matter since all degrees of ability are found. The following tabulation summarizes the findings of the several examinations in the cases of thirty of the most backward cases. The entries give the total number of defects or deficiencies, of the various sorts, found in our appraisal. Several defects or deficiencies may be found in one individual. Which of these are causal we were unable to decide in many instances, as has been indicated above.

It will be understood that the particular groups which have been studied may not include samples of all defects or deficiencies which may contribute to difficulty in reading and spelling. It is likewise unlikely that with another group the same frequencies of defects would be found. It is very probable also that important deficiencies have been missed in our diagnoses and that the diagnoses are often positively erroneous. Finally there is great uncertainty concerning the significance and the interrelations of the defects or deficiencies found. In most cases, while the forms of the difficulty might appear rather clearly, no more than a conjecture at the ultimate cause could be given. No single assumed cause—speech defect, nervousness, poor vision, early training in foreign language—leads, apparently, to any single type of defect, invariably, nor is any type of defect associated invariably with any particular cause.

The investigations conducted and reviewed in this study have disclosed the enormous complexity of reading and spelling as mental functions. However simple the reading or spelling of "cat" may appear, it involves a multiplicity of neural connections and bodily mechanisms whose integrations are so complex that we are unable as yet to present more than a suggestive analysis.

The task of educational diagnosis and treatment is serious business, demanding knowledge and skill that awaits the results of extensive investigation by scientific methods. A case of inability to read affords, frequently, a tangle of difficulties that experts from several professional fields working together may be unable to disentangle. Such a situation portrays clearly the need of a new group of specialists who will make the solution of such problems their main work. It will demand a mastery of the knowledge and technique of several sciences.

Such research is essential, not only because it is plainly desirable to diagnose and remedy the conditions underlying disability, but because the development of general methods of instruction depends upon such knowledge as these achievements would provide. It is folly to expect children to learn functions as complex as reading and spelling economically and effectively without instruction, and it is equally futile to attempt to devise adequate methods of instruction without intimate knowledge of the constituents of these functions and the influence of a variety of factors upon them.

A LIST OF SELECTED REFERENCES

A. GENERAL TREATISES OR SUMMARIES OF EXPERIMENTAL STUDIES

HUEY, E. B. *The Psychology and Pedagogy of Reading.* 469 pp. New York: Macmillan, 1913.

JUDD, C. H. *Reading, Its Nature and Development.* 192 pp. University of Chicago Educational Monographs, Vol. II, No. 4, 1918.

O'BRIEN, JOHN A. *Silent Reading.* 289 pp. New York: Macmillan Co., 1921.

TIDYMAN, W. F. *The Teaching of Spelling.* 178 pp. Yonkers: World Book Co., 1919.

THEISEN, W. W. "Factors Affecting Results in Primary Reading." *Twentieth Yearbook of the National Society for the Study of Education.* Part II, 1921, pp. 1–25.

B. IMPORTANT EXPERIMENTAL INVESTIGATIONS

BUSWELL, G. T. *An Experimental Study of the Eye-voice Span in Reading.* 105 pp. University of Chicago. Sup. Educational Monographs, No. 17, 1920.

DEARBORN, W. F. *The Psychology of Reading.* Columbia University Contributions to Philosophy and Psychology, Vol. 14, No. 1, 1906.

GRAY, C. T. *Types of Reading Ability as Exhibited through Tests and Laboratory Experiments.* 196 pp. University of Chicago, Sup. Educational Monographs, Vol. I, No. 5, 1917.

GRAY, W. S. *Studies of Elementary School Reading through Standardized Tests.* University of Chicago, Sup. Educational Monographs, Vol. I, No. 1, 1917.

HAMILTON, F. M. *The Perceptual Factors in Reading.* 56 pp. Columbia University Contributions to Philosophy and Psychology, Vol. 17, No. 1, 1907.

RUEDIGER, W. C. *The Field of Distinct Vision.* Columbia University Contribution to Philosophy and Psychology, No. 5, 1907.

SCHMIDT, W. A. *An Experimental Study on the Psychology of Reading.* 126 pp. University of Chicago, Sup. Educational Monographs, Vol. I, No. 2, 1917.

C. STUDIES DEALING PRIMARILY WITH READING OR SPELLING DIFFICULTIES

ANDERSON, C. S. and MERTON, ELDA. "Remedial Work in Reading." *Elementary School Journal*, May and June, 1920.

BRONNER, AUGUSTA F. *The Psychology of Special Abilities and Disabilities.* pp. vii + 269. Boston: Little, Brown and Co. 1917.

FERNALD, GRACE M. and KELLER, HELEN. "The Effect of Kinaesthetic Factors in the Development of Word Recognition in the Case of Non-readers." *Journal of Educational Research*, December, 1921.

FILDES, LUCY G. "A Psychological Inquiry into the Nature of the Condition Known as Congenital Word-blindness." *Brain*, November, 1921.

FREEMAN, F. N. "Clinical Study as a Method in Experimental Education." *Journal of Applied Psychology*, June, 1920.

GRAY, W. S. "Individual Difficulties in Silent Reading in the Fourth, Fifth and Sixth Grades." *Twentieth Yearbook of National Society for Study of Education*, 1921, pp. 39–54.

GRAY, W. S. "Diagnostic and Remedial Steps in Reading." *Journal of Educational Research*, June, 1921.

HOLLINGWORTH, L. S. *The Psychology of Special Disability in Spelling.* 105 pp. Teachers College Contributions to Education, No. 88, 1918.

SCHMITT, CLARA. "Developmental Alexia." *Elementary School Journal*, 1918.

THORNDIKE, E. L. "Reading as Reasoning: A Study of Mistakes in Paragraph Reading." *Journal of Educational Psychology*, June, 1917.

UHL, W. L. "The Use of Results of Reading Tests as Bases for Planning Remedial Work." *Elementary School Journal*, December, 1916.

ZIRBES, LAURA. "Diagnostic Measurement as a Basis for Procedure." *Elementary School Journal*, March, 1918.

CPSIA information can be obtained at www.ICGtesting.com
Printed in the USA
LVOW092142241011

251937LV00001B/80/P